PAPERB...

P9-BYU-535

# GOSPEL SONGS

**MELODY LINE, CHORDS AND LYRICS**
**FOR KEYBOARD • GUITAR • VOCAL**

HAL•LEONARD®

ISBN 0-634-00705-X

**HAL•LEONARD®**
CORPORATION
7777 W. BLUEMOUND RD. P.O. BOX 13819 MILWAUKEE, WI 53213

Visit Hal Leonard Online at
**www.halleonard.com**

Welcome to the PAPERBACK SONGS SERIES.

Do you play piano, guitar, electronic keyboard, sing or play any instrument for that matter? If so, this handy "pocket tune" book is for you.

The concise, one-line music notation consists of:

## MELODY, LYRICS & CHORD SYMBOLS

Whether strumming the chords on guitar, "faking" an arrangement on piano/keyboard or singing the lyrics, these fake book style arrangements can be enjoyed at any experience level – hobbyist to professional.

The musical skills necessary to successfully use this book are minimal. If you play guitar and need some help with chords, a basic chord chart is included at the back of the book.

While playing and singing is the first thing that comes to mind when using this book, it can also serve as a compact, comprehensive reference guide.

However you choose to use this PAPERBACK SONGS SERIES book, by all means have fun!

# CONTENTS

*(contents continued)*

# AMAZING GRACE

### Words by JOHN NEWTON
### Traditional American Melody

**Reflectively**

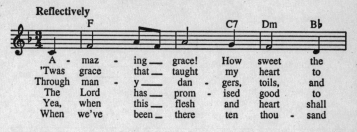

| | | | | | | | |
|---|---|---|---|---|---|---|---|
| A - | maz - | ing | grace! | How | sweet | the | |
| 'Twas | grace | that | taught | my | heart | to | |
| Through | man - | y | dan - | gers, | toils, | and | |
| The | Lord | has | prom - | ised | good | to | |
| Yea, | when | this | flesh | and | heart | shall | |
| When | we've | been | there | ten | thou - | sand | |

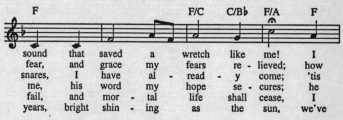

| | | | | | | |
|---|---|---|---|---|---|---|
| sound | that | saved | a | wretch | like | me! I |
| fear, | and | grace | my | fears | re - | lieved; how |
| snares, | I | have | al - | read - | y | come; 'tis |
| me, | his | word | my | hope | se - | cures; he |
| fail, | and | mor - | tal | life | shall | cease, I |
| years, | bright | shin - | ing | as | the | sun, we've |

| | | | | | |
|---|---|---|---|---|---|
| once | was | lost, | but | now | am |
| pre - | cious | did | that | grace | ap - |
| grace | hath | brought | me | safe | thus |
| will | my | shield | and | por - | tion |
| shall | pos - | sess, | with - | in | the |
| no | less | days | to | sing | God's |

| | | | | | | |
|---|---|---|---|---|---|---|
| found; | was | blind, | but | now | I | see. |
| pear | the | hour | I | first | be - | lieved. |
| far, | and | grace | will | lead | me | home. |
| be, | as | long | as | life | en - | dures. |
| veil, | a | life | of | joy | and | peace. |
| praise | than | when | we | first | be - | gun. |

# ANGEL OF DEATH

Words and Music by
HANK WILLIAMS

# ARE YOU WALKIN' AND A-TALKIN' FOR THE LORD

Words and Music by
HANK WILLIAMS

**Brightly**

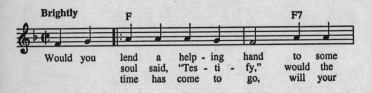

Would you lend a help-ing hand to some
soul said, "Tes-ti-fy," would the
time has come to go, will your

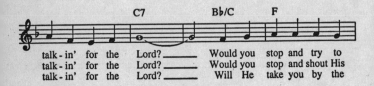

poor sin-ner man, Are you walk-in' and a-
world hear your re-ply, Are you walk-in' and a-
road be white as snow, Are you walk-in' and a-

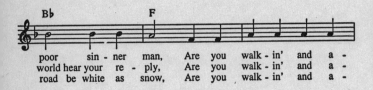

talk-in' for the Lord? _____ Would you stop and try to
talk-in' for the Lord? _____ Would you stop and shout His
talk-in' for the Lord? _____ Will He take you by the

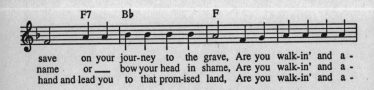

save on your jour-ney to the grave, Are you walk-in' and a-
name or _ bow your head in shame, Are you walk-in' and a-
hand and lead you to that prom-ised land, Are you walk-in' and a-

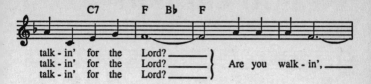

talk - in' for the Lord? _____ }
talk - in' for the Lord? _____ } Are you walk - in', _____
talk - in' for the Lord? _____ }

_____ are you talk - in', _____ Are you walk-in' and a -

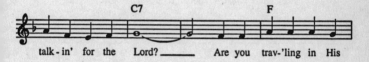

talk - in' for the Lord? _____ Are you trav-'ling in His

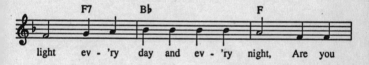

light ev - 'ry day and ev - 'ry night, Are you

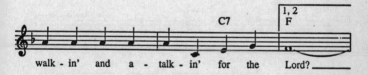

walk - in' and a - talk - in' for the Lord? _____

_____ { If your { When the Lord? _____

# AT CALVARY

Words by WILLIAM NEWELL
Music by D.B. TOWNER

With joy

Years I spent in van - i - ty and pride,
By God's Word at last my sin I learned;
Now I've giv'n to Je - sus ev - 'ry - thing,
O the love that drew sal - va - tion's plan!

Car - ing not my Lord was cru - ci - fied,
Then I trem - bled at the law I'd spurned,
Now I glad - ly own Him as my King,
O the grace that brought it down to man!

Know - ing not it was for me He died on
Till my guilt - y soul im - plor - ing turned to
Now my rap - tured soul can on - ly sing of
O the might - y gulf that God did span at

Cal - va - ry.
Cal - va - ry.
Cal - va - ry.
Cal - va - ry!

Mer - cy there was great and

grace was free, Par - don there was mul - ti -

plied to me, There my bur - dened soul found

lib - er - ty, at Cal - va - ry.

# BECAUSE HE LIVES

Words by WILLIAM J. and GLORIA GAITHER
Music by WILLIAM J. GAITHER

**Moderately**

God sent His Son, _____ They called Him
hold _____ our new - born
day _____ I'll cross the

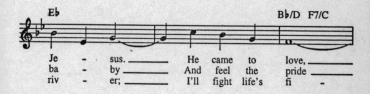

Je - sus. _____ He came to love,
ba - by. _____ And feel the pride
riv - er; _____ I'll fight life's fi -

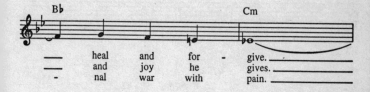

_____ heal and for - give. _____
_____ and joy he gives. _____
- nal war with pain. _____

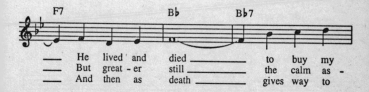

_____ He lived and died _____ to buy my
_____ But great - er still _____ the calm as -
_____ And then as death _____ gives way to

14

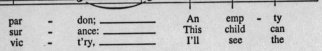

par - don; _____ An emp - ty
sur - ance: _____ This child can
vic - t'ry, _____ I'll see the

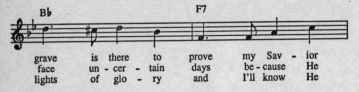

grave is there to prove my Sav - ior
face un - cer - tain days be - cause He
lights of glo - ry and I'll know He

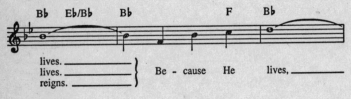

lives. _____
lives. _____ } Be - cause He lives, _____
reigns. _____

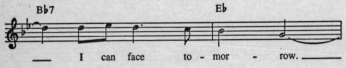

_____ I can face to - mor - row. _____

_____ Be - cause He lives, _____ All fear is

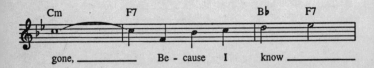

gone, _____ Be - cause I know _____

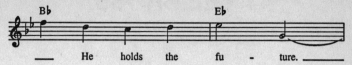

He holds the fu - ture. _____

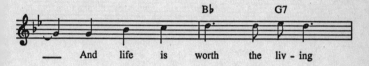

_____ And life is worth the liv - ing

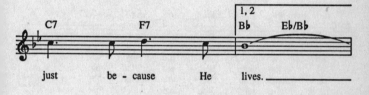

just be - cause He lives. _____

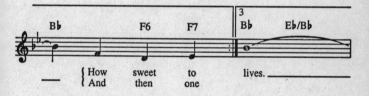

{ How sweet to lives. _____
{ And then one

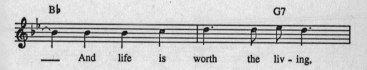

_____ And life is worth the liv - ing,

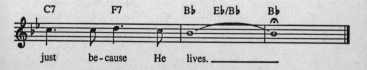

just be - cause He lives. _____

# AT THE CROSS

Text by ISAAC WATTS
Music by RALPH E. HUDSON

**Moderately**

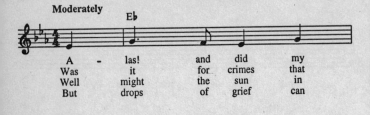

A - las! and did my
Was it for crimes that
Well might the sun in
But drops of grief can

Sav - ior bleed? And did my Sov - 'reign
I have done He suf - fered on the
dark - ness hide And shut His glo - ries
ne'er re - pay The debt of love I

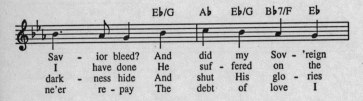

die? Would He de - vote that
tree? A - maz - ing pit - y!
in, When Christ, the might - y
owe. Here, Lord, I give my -

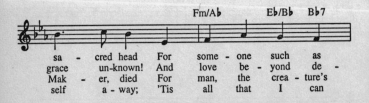

sa - cred head For some - one such as
grace un-known! And love be - yond de -
Mak - er, died For man, the crea - ture's
self a - way; 'Tis all that I can

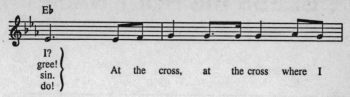

At the cross, at the cross where I

first ____ saw the light And the

bur - den of my heart rolled a -

way; It was there by faith I re -

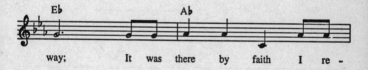

ceived my ____ sight, and

now I am hap - py all the day!

# BLESS HIS HOLY NAME

### Words and Music by ANDRAÉ CROUCH

things, _____ He has done great

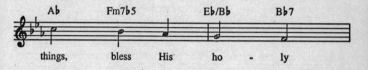

things, bless His ho - ly

name. Bless the Lord,

O my soul, and all that is with -

in me, bless His ho -

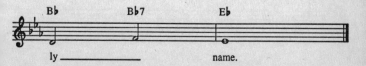

ly _____ name.

# BLESSED ASSURANCE

Lyrics by FANNY CROSBY and VAN ALSTYNE
Music by PHOEBE P. KNAPP

# DADDY SANG BASS

### Words and Music by CARL PERKINS

I re-mem-ber when I was a lad, times were
mem-ber af-ter work, Ma-ma would

hard and things were bad; But there's a
call in all of us; you could

sil-ver lin-ing be-hind ev-'ry cloud.
hear us sing-in' for a coun-try mile.

Just poor peo-ple, that's all we
Now, lit-tle broth-er has done gone

were, try'n' to make a liv-in' out of black land
on, but I'll re-join him in a

22

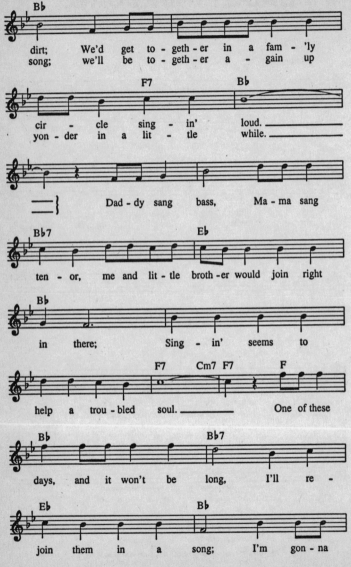

# THE BLOOD WILL NEVER LOSE ITS POWER

### Words and Music by ANDRAÉ CROUCH

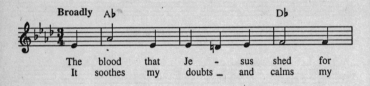

Broadly    Ab                                      Db

The    blood    that    Je  -  sus    shed    for
It    soothes    my    doubts  _  and    calms    my

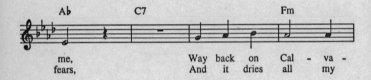

Ab          C7                          Fm

me,              Way    back    on    Cal  -  va  -
fears,           And    it    dries    all    my

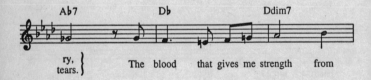

Ab7              Db                  Ddim7

ry, }
tears. }           The    blood    that gives me strength    from

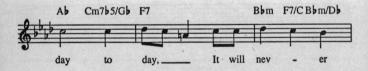

Ab  Cm7b5/Gb  F7                  Bbm  F7/C Bbm/Db

day        to        day, _____    It    will    nev  -  er

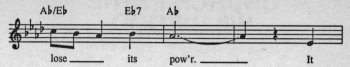

lose _____ its pow'r. _____ It

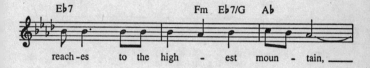

reach -es to the high - est moun - tain, _____

_____ It flows to the low - est

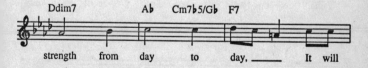

val - ley; _____ The blood that gives me

strength from day to day, _____ It will

nev - er lose _____ its pow'r. _____

# CHURCH IN THE WILDWOOD

### Words and Music by WILLIAM S. PITTS

**Moderately**

There's a church in the val-ley by the wild - wood, no
come to the church _ in the wild - wood, to the
church in the val-ley by the wild - wood, when

love - li - er spot in the dale. No _ where the
trees where the wild flow - ers bloom, where the I would
day fades a - way in - to night, I would

place is so dear to my child - hood as the
part - ing _ hymn will be chant - ed; we will
fain from this spot of my child - hood; wing - ing

lit - tle brown church in the vale. }
weep _ by the side of the tomb. } Oh, _
way _ to the man - sions of light. }

come, come, come, come. Come to the church in the

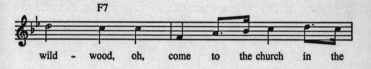

wild - wood, oh, come to the church in the

vale. No ____ place is so dear to my

child - hood as the lit - tle brown church in the

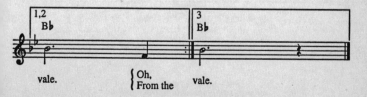

vale. { Oh, / From the } vale.

# THE DAY HE WORE MY CROWN

Words and Music by PHIL JOHNSON

Reflectively

C ... Em7

The cit - y was Je - ru - sa - lem,
He brought me love that on-ly He could give.
But he walked right through the gate

G/F    Fmaj7    Gsus    G

the time was long a - go.
I brought Him cause to cry.
and then on up the hill.

C    Em7

The peo - ple called Him Je - sus,
And though He taught me how to live,
And as He fell be - neath the weight,

G/F    Fmaj7    Gsus    G

the crime was the love He showed.
I taught Him how to die.
He cried, "Fa - ther, not my will."

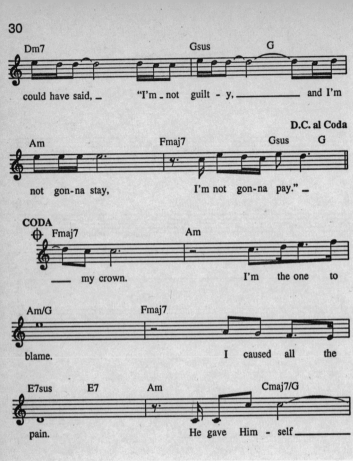

Dm7 | Gsus | G

could have said, — "I'm — not guilt - y, ————— and I'm

Am | Fmaj7 | Gsus | G

**D.C. al Coda**

not gon-na stay, I'm not gon-na pay." —

**CODA**

Fmaj7 | Am

— my crown. I'm the one to

Am/G | Fmaj7

blame. I caused all the

E7sus | E7 | Am | Cmaj7/G

pain. He gave Him - self ————

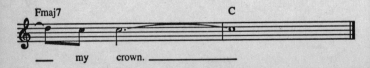

Fmaj7 | Gsus | G7

————— the day He wore —————

Fmaj7 | C

— my crown. —————

# DO LORD

### Traditional

I've got a home in glo-ry land that out-shines the sun,
I took Je-sus as my Sav-ior; you take Him, too.

I've got a home in glo-ry land that out-shines the sun,
I took Je-sus as my Sav-ior; you take Him, too.

I've got a home in glo-ry land that out-shines the sun,
I took Je-sus as my Sav-ior; you take Him, too,

Way be-yond the blue.
While He's call-ing you.
Do Lord, O do Lord, O

do re-mem-ber me. Do Lord, O do Lord, O

do re-mem-ber me. Do Lord, O do Lord, O

do re-mem-ber me, way be-yond the blue.

# DEAR BROTHER

Words and Music by
HANK WILLIAMS

Reflectively

Dear Broth-er, Ma-ma left us this
stood by her bed-side those last few

morn-ing, Yes, the an-gels took her a-
mo-ments, I lived my child-hood a-

way. She's gone to meet
gain. I thought of you,

Dad-dy up there in heav-en, But
Broth-er, and of the old home-stead; And my

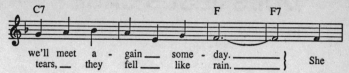

we'll meet a - gain___ some - day.___
tears,___ they fell___ like rain.___ } She

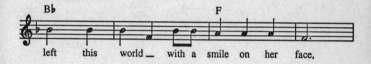

left this world___ with a smile on her face,

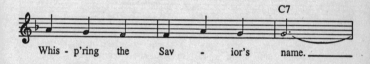

Whis - p'ring the Sav - ior's name. ___

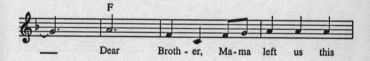

___ Dear Broth - er, Ma - ma left us this

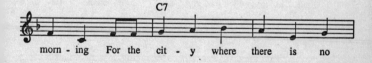

morn - ing For the cit - y where there is no

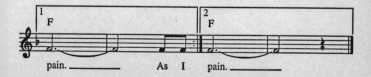

pain. ___ As I pain. ___

# DOES JESUS CARE?

Words by FRANK E. GRAEFF
Music by J. LINCOLN HALL

Does Je - sus care when my
Does Je - sus care when my
Does Je - sus care when I've
Does Je - sus care when I've

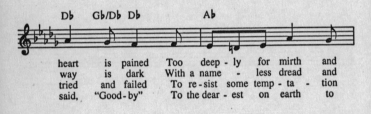

heart is pained Too deep - ly for mirth and
way is dark With a name - less dread and
tried and failed To re - sist some temp - ta - tion
said, "Good - by" To the dear - est on earth to

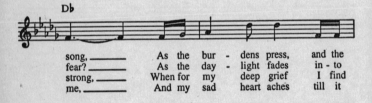

song, _____ As the bur - dens press, and the
fear? _____ As the day - light fades in - to
strong, _____ When for my deep grief I find
me, _____ And my sad heart aches till it

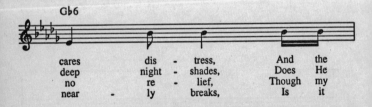

cares dis - tress, And the
deep night - shades, Does He
no re - lief, Though my
near - ly breaks, Is it

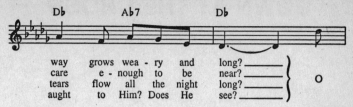

way    grows wea - ry  and   long? _____
care    e - nough   to   be   near? _____
tears   flow  all  the   night  long? _____
aught  to Him? Does He   see? _____

O

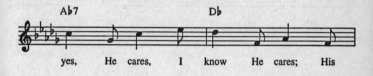

yes,    He  cares,    I    know    He  cares;   His

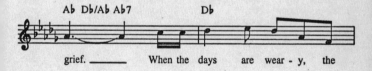

heart        is    touched    with    my

grief. _____    When the days  are wear - y,  the

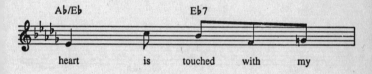

long    nights    drear - y,    I

know   my   Sav - ior   cares. _____

# DOWN AT THE CROSS

Words by ELISHA A. HOFFMAN
Music by JOHN H. STOCKTON

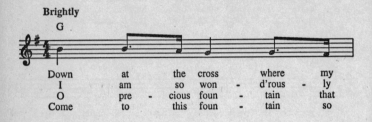

Brightly

Down      at      the  cross      where      my
I      am      so   won  -  d'rous  -  ly
O      pre  -  cious  foun  -  tain      that
Come      to      this  foun  -  tain      so

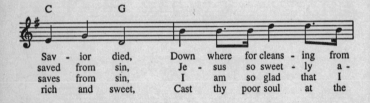

Sav  -  ior   died,      Down  where  for  cleans  -  ing  from
saved  from   sin,      Je  -  sus  so  sweet  -  ly  a  -
saves  from   sin,      I      am  so  glad  that   I
rich   and   sweet,      Cast  thy  poor  soul  at  the

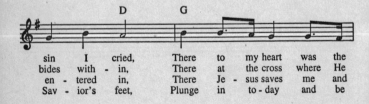

sin      I   cried,      There   to   my  heart  was   the
bides  with  -  in,      There   at  the  cross  where  He
en  -  tered   in,      There   Je  -  sus  saves  me  and
Sav  -  ior's  feet,      Plunge  in   to - day  and   be

blood ap - plied; )
took me in; )
keeps me clean; ) Glo - ry to His
made com - plete; )

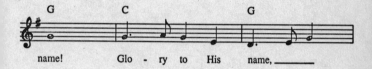

name! Glo - ry to His name, _____

Glo - ry to His name! _____

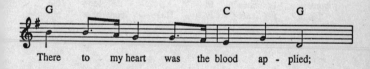

There to my heart was the blood ap - plied;

Glo - ry to His name!

# DWELLING IN BEULAH LAND

### Words and Music by C. AUSTIN MILES

Far a-way the noise of strife up-
Far be-low the storm of doubt up-
Let the storm-y breez-es blow, their
View-ing here the works of God, I

on my ear is fall-ing,
on the world is beat-ing,
cry can-not a-larm me,
sink in con-tem-pla-tion,

Then I know the sins of earth be-
Sons of men in bat-tle long the
I am safe-ly shel-tered here pro-
Hear-ing now His bless-ed voice, I

set on ev-'ry hand;
en-e-my with-stand;
tect-ed by God's hand;
see the way He planned;

**Bb**

Doubt and fear and things of earth in
Safe am I with - in the cas - tle
Here the sun is al - ways shin - ing,
Dwell - ing in the Spir - it, here I

**Bb/F**   **F7**   **Bb**

vain to me are call - ing,
of God's Word re - treat - ing,
here there's naught can harm me,
learn of full sal - va - tion,

**Eb**   **Bb/F**   **Eb**

None of these shall move me from
Noth - ing then can reach me, 'tis
I am safe for - ev - er in
Glad - ly will I tar - ry in

**Bb/F**   **F7**   **Bb**

Beu - lah Land.
Beu - lah Land.
Beu - lah Land.
Beu - lah Land.

I'm

liv - ing on the moun - tain, un - der-

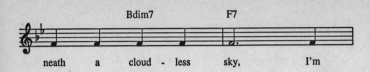

neath a cloud - less sky, I'm

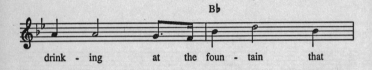

drink - ing at the foun - tain that

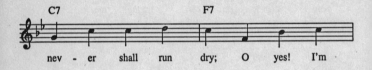

nev - er shall run dry; O yes! I'm

feast - ing on the man - na from a

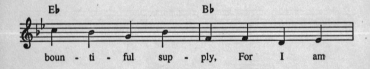

boun - ti - ful sup - ply, For I am

dwell - ing in Beu - lah Land.

# FOR THOSE TEARS I DIED <sup>41</sup>

Words and Music by MARSHA J. STEVENS

**With feeling**

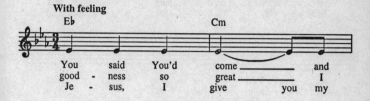

You said You'd come _____ and
good - ness so great _____ I
Je - sus, I give you my

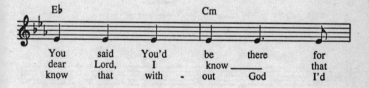

share all my sor - rows, _____
can't un - der - stand, _____ and
heart and my soul, _____ I

You said You'd be there for
dear Lord, I know _____ that
know that with - out God I'd

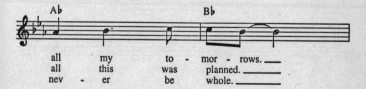

all my to - mor - rows. _____
all this was planned. _____
nev - er be whole. _____

# THE EASTERN GATE

Words and Music by I.G. MARTIN

Moderately

I will meet you in the morn — ing,
If you has-ten off to glo — ry,
Keep your lamps all trimmed and burn — ing,
O the joy of that glad meet — ing

Just in - side the East-ern Gate.
Lin - ger near the East-ern Gate;
For the Bride-groom watch and wait.
With the saints who for us wait!

Then be read - y, faith-ful pil — grim,
For I'm com - ing in the morn — ing,
He'll be with us at the meet — ing,
What a bless - ed hap - py meet — ing,

Lest with you it be too late.
So you'll not have long to wait.
Just in - side the East-ern Gate!
Just in - side the East-ern Gate!

I will

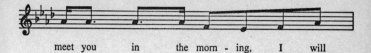

meet you in the morn - ing, I will

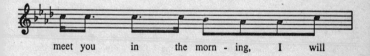

meet you in the morn-ing Just in - side the East-ern Gate o - ver

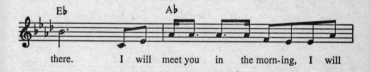

there. I will meet you in the morn-ing, I will

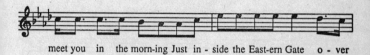

meet you in the morn - ing, I will

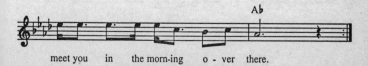

meet you in the morn-ing o - ver there.

# THE FAMILY OF GOD

Words by WILLIAM J. and GLORIA GAITHER
Music by WILLIAM J. GAITHER

I'm so glad I'm a part of the fam - 'ly of God; I've been washed in the foun - tain, cleansed by His blood! Joint heirs with Je - sus as we trav - el this sod, For I'm part of the fam - 'ly, the fam - 'ly of God.

You will
From the

no - tice    we say broth - er ⌒ and
door ⌒ of an orph - 'nage to the

**C7**

sis - ter ⌒ 'round here. It's be - cause we're a
house of ⌒ the King. No ⌒ long - er an

**F**    **Bb**

fam - 'ly ⌒ and these folks are so
out - cast, ⌒ a ⌒ new song I

**F**

near. When one has a heart - ache ⌒ we ⌒
sing. From rags un - to rich - es, ⌒ from the

**Bb**    **F**      **C7**

all share the tears, And re - joice in each
weak to the strong, I'm not worth - y to

**Gm7**      **C7**

vic - t'ry ⌒ in this fam - 'ly so
be ⌒ here ⌒ but praise God I be -

**F**    **Bb/F**    **|1.** **F**      **|2.** **F**      **D.S. al Coda**

dear. ⌒ I'm so
long! ⌒ I'm so

**CODA**
**Gm7**      **C7**      **F**

fam - 'ly of God.

# FILL MY CUP, LORD

Words and Music by RICHARD BLANCHARD

**Reflectively**

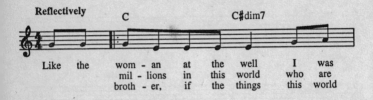

Like the wom - an at the well I was
mil - lions in this world who are
broth - er, if the things this world

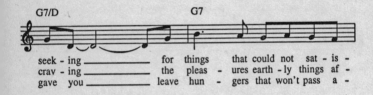

seek - ing _____ for things that could not sat - is -
crav - ing _____ the pleas - ures earth - ly things af -
gave you _____ leave hun - gers that won't pass a -

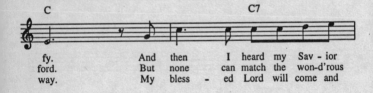

fy. And then I heard my Sav - ior
ford. But none can match the won - d'rous
way. My bless - ed Lord will come and

speak - ing: _____ "Draw from My I
treas - ure _____ that I
save you _____ if you

49

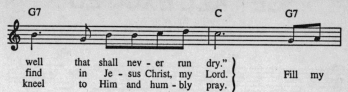

well that shall nev - er run dry."  
find in Je - sus Christ, my Lord.  
kneel to Him and hum - bly pray. Fill my

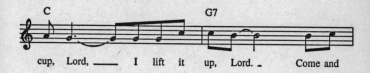

cup, Lord, ____ I lift it up, Lord. _ Come and

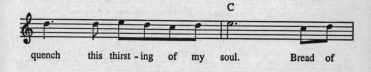

quench this thirst - ing of my soul. Bread of

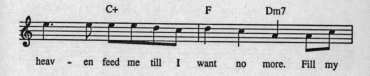

heav - en feed me till I want no more. Fill my

cup, fill it up and make me

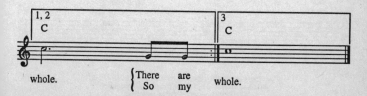

whole.  
There are  
So my  
whole.

# GET ALL EXCITED

### Words and Music by
### WILLIAM J. GAITHER

51

# GIVE ME THAT OLD TIME RELIGION

Traditional

# GIVE UP

## Words and Music by HOWARD GOODMAN

Slow, Gospel feel

Give up and let Je - sus take o - ver, _____ Give up and let Je - sus take o - ver, _____ Give up and let Je - sus take

# GIVE THEM ALL TO JESUS

Words and Music by BOB BENSON SR. and PHIL JOHNSON

**Flowing**

Are you tired of chas - in' ___ pret - ty rain - bows, and are you tired of spin - nin' 'round and 'round? ___

He nev - er said ___ you'd on - ly see sun - shine, and He nev - er said ___ there'd be no rain. ___

Wrap up all the shat - tered dreams ___ of your ___ life ___ and at the feet of Je -

He ___ on - ly prom - ised a heart full of sing - ing ___ a - bout the ver - y things ___

# GOD BLESS THE U.S.A.

Words and Music by
LEE GREENWOOD

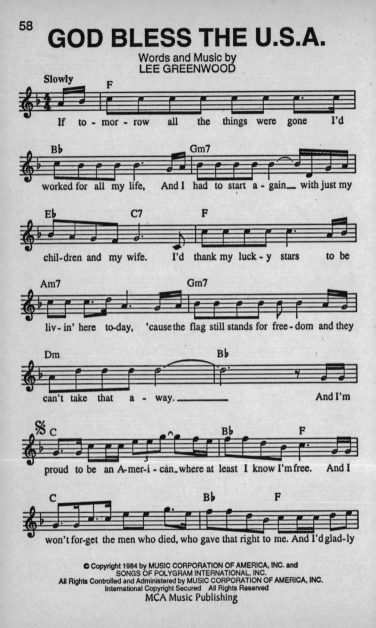

MCA Music Publishing

60

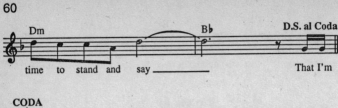

Dm ⌢ Bb          D.S. al Coda

time    to    stand    and    say _____    That I'm

**CODA**

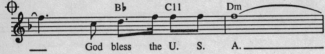

Dm          Bb    C11    Dm

___    God    bless    the    U.    S.    A. _____

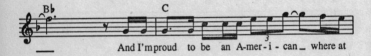

Bb          C

___    And I'm proud    to be    an A-mer-i-can ___ where at

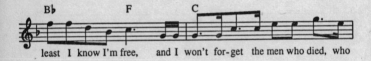

Bb          F          C

least    I    know    I'm free,    and I    won't for-get    the men who died,    who

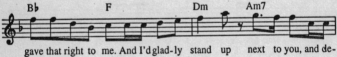

Bb          F          Dm    Am7

gave    that right    to me.    And I'd glad-ly    stand    up    next    to you, and de-

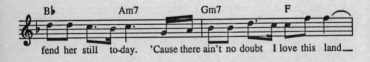

Bb          Am7          Gm7          F

fend    her still    to-day.    'Cause there ain't    no doubt    I love this    land ___

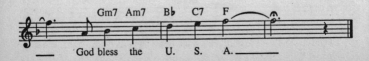

Gm7    Am7    Bb    C7    F

___    God    bless    the    U.    S.    A. _____

# GOD WILL TAKE CARE OF YOU

Words by CIVILLA D. MARTIN
Music by W. STILLMAN MARTIN

# HALLELUJAH, WE SHALL RISE

### By J.E. THOMAS

**Joyfully**

In the res - ur - rec - tion morn - ing, when the
res - ur - rec - tion morn - ing, what a
res - ur - rec - tion morn - ing, bless - ed
res - ur - rec - tion morn - ing, we shall

We shall rise,

trump of God shall sound,
meet - ing it will be!
thought it is to me;
meet Him in the air.

Hal - le - lu - jah! we shall

rise.

Then the saints will come re - joic - ing and no
When our fa - thers and our moth - ers and our
I shall see my bless - ed Sav - ior, who so
And be car - ried up to glo - ry, to our

We shall rise,                    we shall

tears will e'er be found.
loved ones we shall see!
free - ly died for me.
home so bright and fair.

We shall rise, hal - le - lu - jah! in the

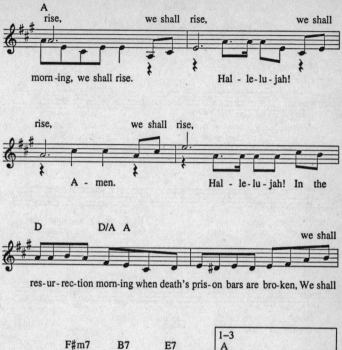

A
rise, we shall rise, we shall
morn-ing, we shall rise. Hal - le - lu - jah!

rise, we shall rise,
A - men. Hal - le - lu - jah! In the

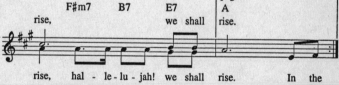

D  D/A  A  we shall
res-ur-rec-tion morn-ing when death's pris-on bars are bro-ken, We shall

F#m7  B7  E7  1–3  A
rise, we shall rise.
rise, hal - le - lu - jah! we shall rise. In the

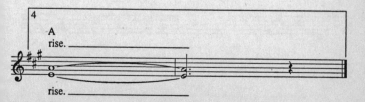

4
A
rise. _____
rise. _____

# HE

Words by RICHARD MULLEN
Music by JACK RICHARDS

**Moderately slow**

He ____ can turn the tides ____ and calm the
He ____ can grant a wish ____ or make a

an - gry sea, He ____ a - lone de -
dream come true, He ____ can paint the

cides ____ who writes a sym - pho - ny;
clouds ____ and turn the gray to blue;

He ____ lights ev - 'ry star ____ that makes our
He ____ a - lone knows where ____ to find the

dark - ness bright, He ____ keeps watch all
rain - bow's end, He ____ a - lone can

# HE LOVED ME WITH A CROSS

### Words and Music by JOEL LINDSEY and SUE SMITH

**Tenderly**

You left a throne in heav - en _____ to
He knew from the be - gin - ning _____ the

come to Beth - le - hem,
price He'd have to pay, for my

I will not for - get the way He
heart had gone so far be - yond what

loved me e - ven then;
oth - er loves for - gave;

And ev - 'ry -where He trav - eled _____ He
I was - n't on that hill - side _____ to

68

# HE'S GOT THE WHOLE
# WORLD IN HIS HANDS

### African-American Folksong

# HE TOUCHED ME

### Words and Music by WILLIAM J. GAITHER

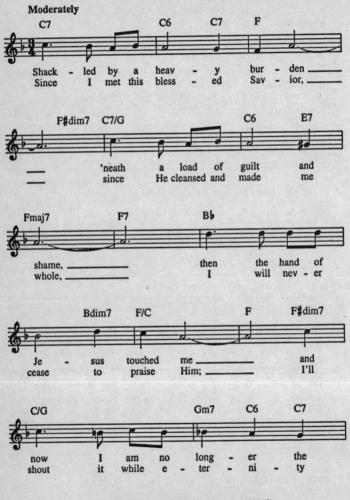

Moderately

Shack - led by a heav - y bur - den
Since I met this bless - ed Sav - ior,

'neath a load of guilt and
since He cleansed and made me

shame, then the hand of
whole, I will nev - er

Je - sus touched me and
cease to praise Him; I'll

now I am no long - er the
shout it while e - ter - ni - ty

71

same. ——— } He touched me, ——
rolls. ——— }

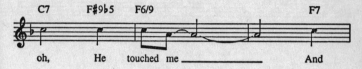

oh, He touched me ——————— And

oh, the joy that floods my

soul. ——— Some - thing ——

hap - pened ——— and now I know He

touched me —— and made —— me whole. ———

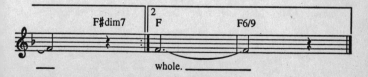

—— whole. ———

# HELP ME UNDERSTAND

Words and Music by
HANK WILLIAMS

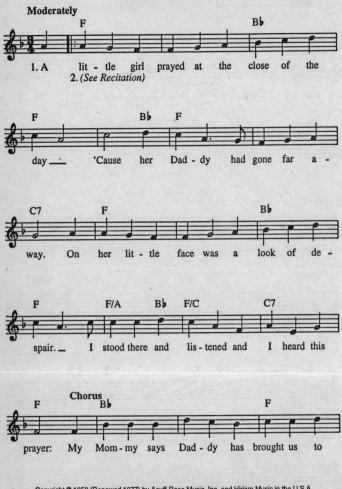

Moderately

1. A lit - tle girl prayed at the close of the
2. (See Recitation)

day ___ 'Cause her Dad - dy had gone far a -

way. On her lit - tle face was a look of de -

spair. ___ I stood there and lis - tened and I heard this

Chorus

prayer: My Mom - my says Dad - dy has brought us to

shame, __ I'm nev - er no more __ to men - tion his name. Lord, take me and lead me and hold to my hand. __ Oh, Heav - en - ly Fa - ther, help me un - der - stand. me un - der - stand.

### Recitation

You know, Friends, I wonder how many homes are broken tonight -
  just how many tears are shed
By some little word of anger that never should have been said.
I'd like to tell you a story of a family I once knew.
We'll call them Mary and William and their little daughter, Sue.
Mary was just a plain Mother, and Bill - well, he was the usual Dad,
And they had their family quarrels, like everyone else - but neither one got mad.
Then one day something happened - it was nothing, of course,
But one word led to another, and the last word led to a divorce.


Now here were two grown up people who failed to see common sense.
They strengthened their own selfish pride at little Sue's expense.
You know, she didn't ask to be brought into this world, to drift from pillar to post,
But a divorce never stops to consider the one it hurts the most.
There'd be a lot more honest lovin' in this wicked world today
If just a few parted parents could hear little Sue say:
*Chorus*

# HIGHER GROUND

**Words by JOHNSON OATMAN, JR.**
**Music by CHARLES H. GABRIEL**

Moderately

I'm press-ing on the up-ward way, New heights I'm
live a-bove the world, Though Sa-tan's
scale the ut-most height And catch a

gain-ing ev-'ry day; Still pray-ing
darts at me are hurled; For faith has
gleam of glo-ry bright; But still I'll

as I on-ward bound, "Lord, plant my feet on high-er
caught the joy-ful sound, the song of saints on high-er
pray till heav'n I've found, "Lord, lead me on to high-er

ground." } Lord, lift me up and let me
ground.
ground."

stand, By faith on heav-en's ta-ble-

land; A high-er plane than I have found, Lord, plant my

feet on high-er ground. I want to ground.

1, 2

3

# HOLY GROUND

**Words and Music by GERON DAVIS**

76

# HIS EYE IS ON
# THE SPARROW

### Text by CIVILLA D. MARTIN
### Music by CHARLES H. GABRIEL

eye     is     on \_\_\_\_ the     spar - row, \_\_\_\_     And I

know     He     watch - es     me; \_\_\_\_     His

eye     is     on     the     spar - row, \_\_\_\_     And I

know     He     watch - es     me. \_\_\_\_     I

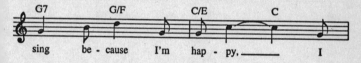

sing     be - cause     I'm     hap - py, \_\_\_\_     I

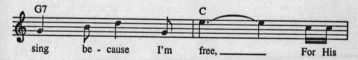

sing     be - cause     I'm     free, \_\_\_\_     For His

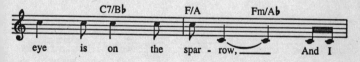

eye     is     on     the     spar - row, \_\_\_\_     And I

know     He     watch - es     me.

# HIS NAME IS WONDERFUL

Words and Music by AUDREY MIEIR

His name is Won-der-ful, Je - sus, my

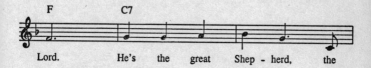

Lord. He's the great Shep - herd, the

Rock of all a - ges, Al - might - y

God is He.

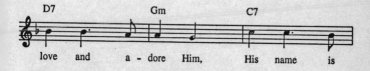

Bow down be - fore Him,

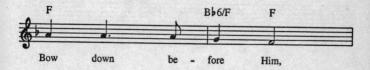

love and a - dore Him, His name is

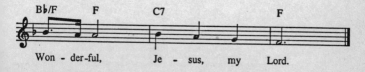

Won - der - ful, Je - sus, my Lord.

# HOLY IS HIS NAME

### Words and Music by JOHN MICHAEL TALBOT

**With conviction**

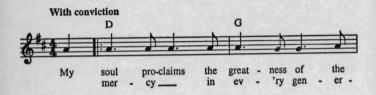

My soul pro-claims the great - ness of the
mer - cy ___ in ev - 'ry gen - er -

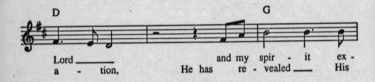

Lord ___ and my spir - it ex -
a - tion, He has re - vealed ___ His

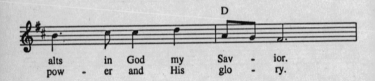

alts in God my Sav - ior.
pow - er and His glo - ry.

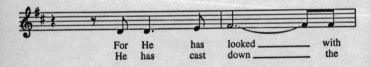

For He has looked ___ with
He has cast down ___ the

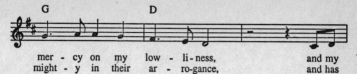

mer - cy on my low - li - ness,
and my
might - y in their ar - ro-gance,
and has

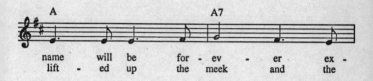

name will be for - ev - er ex -
lift - ed up the meek and the

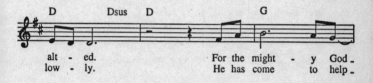

alt - ed.
For the might - y God
low - ly.
He has come to help

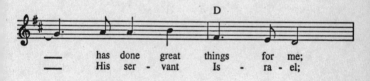

has done great things for me;
His ser - vant Is - ra - el;

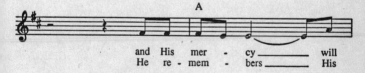

and His mer - cy will
He re - mem - bers His

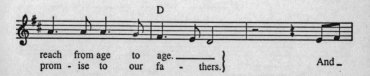

reach from age to age.
And
prom - ise to our fa - thers.

Ho - ly, Ho -

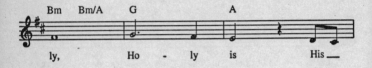

ly, Ho - ly is His ___

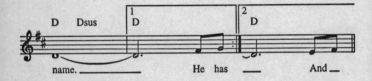

name. ___ He has ___ And ___

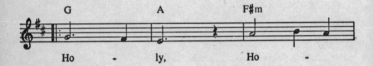

Ho - ly, Ho -

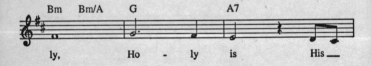

ly, Ho - ly is His ___

name. ___ And ___ ___

# HOME WHERE I BELONG

Words and Music by PAT TERRY

They say that heav-en's pret-ty, and
Some-times when I'm dream-in', it
When I'm feel-in' lone-ly and

liv-in' here is, too. But
comes as no sur-prise that
when I'm feel-in' blue, it's

if they said that I would have to choose
if you'll look you'll see the home-sick feel-
such a joy to know that I am on-

be-tween the two, I'd go home,
-in' in my eyes. I'm go-in' home,
-ly pass-in' through. I'm head-ed home,

go-in' home,
I'm go-in' home,
I'm go-in' home,

86

# A HOME IN HEAVEN

Words and Music by
HANK WILLIAMS

**Moderately**

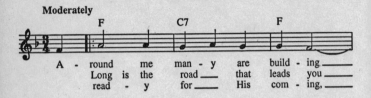

A - round me man-y are build - ing ___
Long is the road ___ that leads you ___
read - y for ___ His com - ing, ___

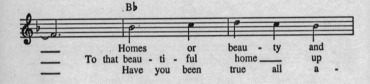

___ Homes or beau - ty and
To that beau - ti - ful home ___ up
Have you been true all a -

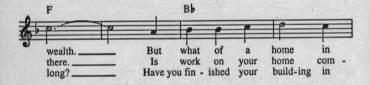

wealth. ___ But what of a home in
there. ___ Is work on your home com -
long? ___ Have you fin - ished your build-ing in

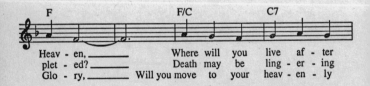

Heav - en, ___ Where will you live af - ter
plet - ed? ___ Death may be ling - er - ing
Glo - ry, ___ Will you move to your heav - en - ly

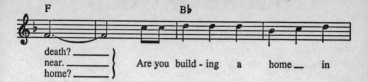

death? _____
near. _____
home? _____

Are you build-ing a home _ in

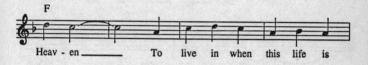

Heav-en _____ To live in when this life is

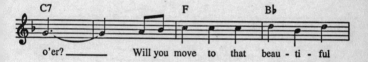

o'er? _____ Will you move to that beau-ti-ful

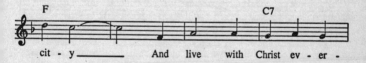

cit-y _____ And live with Christ ev-er-

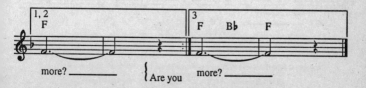

more? _____ { Are you more? _____

# HOUSE OF GOLD

Words and Music by
HANK WILLIAMS

# I BOWED ON MY KNEES
# AND CRIED HOLY

Words by NETTIE DUDLEY WASHINGTON
Music by E.M. DUDLEY CANTWELL

92

# HOW CAN YOU REFUSE HIM NOW

### Words and Music by
### HANK WILLIAMS

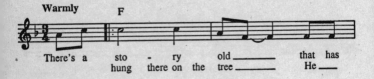

There's a sto - ry old _____ that has
hung there on the tree _____ He _____

of - ten been told _____ Of how our
prayed for you and me; _____ There was no one His

Sav - ior died. _____ As they nailed His
pain _____ to ease. _____ Be - fore He

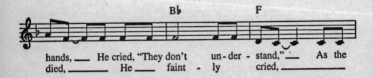

hands, _____ He cried, "They don't un - der - stand," _____ As the
died, _____ He _____ faint - ly cried, _____

**C7**      **F**   **Bb**   **F**

blood    flowed    from    his    side. _____
"Fa - ther, for - give    them,    please." _____ }    How can

**Bb**                   **F**

you    re - fuse Him   now,    how can   you    re - fuse Him

                                 **Gm7**     **C7**

now,  How can  you    turn a - way  from His   side? _____    With

**F**                                 **Bb**

tears    in His   eyes, _____    on the   cross    there He

**F**                                 **C7**

died; _____   How can  you    re - fuse   Je - sus

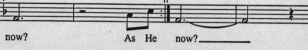

 1                                 2
**F**       **C7**                   **F**   **Bb Bbm6 F**

now?                   As He   now? _____

# HOW GREAT THOU ART

Words and Music by STUART K. HINE

*Also "worlds" and "rolling"

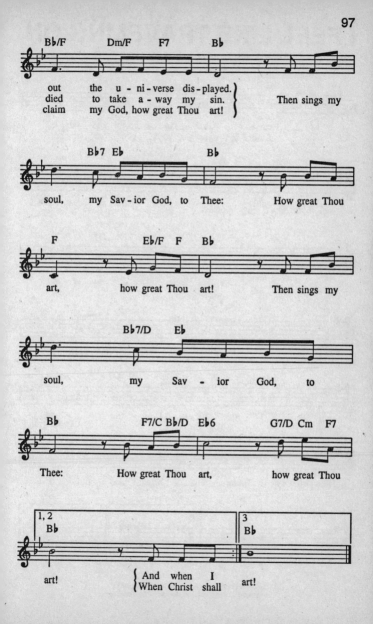

# I FEEL LIKE TRAVELING ON

### Words and Music by WILLIAM HUNTER

With movement

My__ Heav-en-ly home__ is__ bright and fair} I
Lord__ has been__ so__ good to me

feel like trav-el-ing on. {No__ pain or death__ can__
Un__til that bless__ed__

en__ter there} I feel like__ trav-el-ing
home I see

on. Yes, I feel like trav-el-ing

on. I feel like trav-el-ing on. My__

Heav-en-ly home__ is__ bright and fair I

feel like__ trav-el-ing on. My__ on.

# I JUST CAME TO PRAISE THE LORD

### Words and Music by WAYNE ROMERO

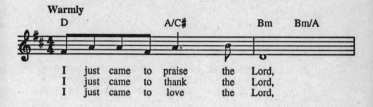

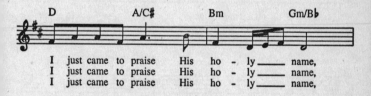

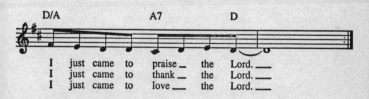

# I JUST FEEL LIKE SOMETHING GOOD IS ABOUT TO HAPPEN

### Words and Music by WILLIAM J. GAITHER

# I SAW THE LIGHT

**Words and Music by HANK WILLIAMS**

# I WOULDN'T TAKE NOTHING FOR MY JOURNEY NOW

Words and Music by JIMMIE DAVIS
and CHARLES F. GOODMAN

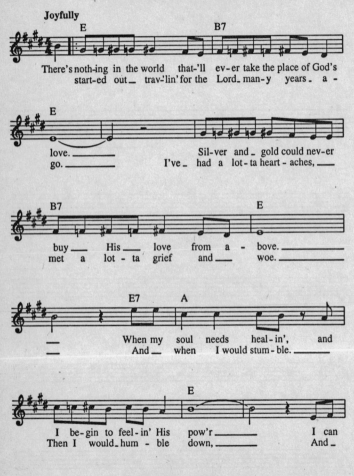

**Joyfully**

There's noth-ing in the world that'll ev-er take the place of God's
start-ed out_ trav-'lin' for the Lord_ man-y years_ a-

love._ Sil-ver and_ gold could nev-er
go._ I've_ had a lot-ta heart-aches,_

buy_ His_ love from a- bove._
met a lot-ta grief and_ woe._

When my soul needs heal-in', and
And_ when I would stum-ble._

I be-gin to feel-in' His pow'r_ I can
Then I would-hum-ble down,_ And_

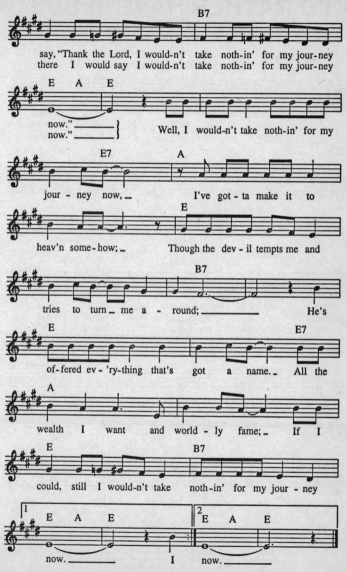

say, "Thank the Lord, I would-n't take noth-in' for my jour-ney
there I would say I would-n't take noth-in' for my jour-ney

now."
now."
} Well, I would-n't take noth-in' for my

jour - ney now, — I've got-ta make it to

heav'n some-how; — Though the dev - il tempts me and

tries to turn — me a - round; — He's

of-fered ev-'ry-thing that's got a name. — All the

wealth I want and world - ly fame; — If I

could, still I would-n't take noth-in' for my jour - ney

1. now. — I

2. now. —

# I'D RATHER HAVE JESUS

Words by RHEA F. MILLER
Music by GEORGE BEVERLY SHEA

**Thoughtfully**

I'd rath - er have Je - sus than
rath - er have Je - sus than
fair - er than lil - ies of

sil - ver or gold, I'd rath - er be
men's ap - plause, I'd rath - er be
rar - est___ bloom, He's sweet - er than

His than have rich - es un - told, I'd
faith - ful to His___ dear cause, I'd
hon - ey from out___ the comb, He's

rath - er have Je - sus than hous - es or
rath - er have Je - sus than world - wide___
all that my hun - ger - ing spir - it___

lands. I'd rath - er be led by His
fame. I'd rath - er be true to His
needs. I'd rath - er have Je - sus and

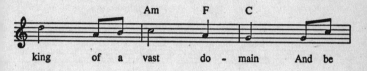

nail - pierced hand }
ho - ly name } Than to be the
let Him lead }

king of a vast do - main And be

held in sin's dread sway. _____ I'd

rath - er have Je - sus than an - y -

thing This __ world af - fords to -

1, 2    3

day. _____ { I'd
        { He's  day. _____

# I'LL FLY AWAY

### Words and Music by ALBERT E. BRUMLEY

# IN THE GARDEN

### Words and Music by C. AUSTIN MILES

**Tenderly**

I come to the gar-den a-lone_____ while the
He speaks, and the sound of His voice_____ is so
I'd stay in the gar-den with Him_____ though the

dew is still on the ros - es, And the
sweet the birds hush their sing - ing, And the
night a-round me be fall - ing, But He

voice I hear fall-ing on my ear, The Son of God dis-
mel-o-dy that He gave to me With-in my heart is
bids me go; thru the voice of woe His voice to me is

clos - es.)
ring - ing.} And He walks with me, and He talks with me, and He
call - ing.)

tells me I am His own;____ and the joy we share as we

tar-ry there, none oth-er has ev-er____ known.__

# IN THE PRESENCE OF JEHOVAH

### Words and Music by GERON DAVIS
### and BECKY DAVIS

**Worshipfully**

Ab/Db    Db

In and out of___ sit - u - a        tions ___

Db/F        Gb

___    that tug - of - war at me,

Ab9sus        Ab/Db        Db

all day long I strug - gle ___

Db/F        Gb

___    for an - swers that I need.

Bb7/F        Ebsus4(add2)    Ebm

But, then I come in - to His pres - ence

Ab7        Ab/Gb        Db/F        F7/A

and all my ques - tions ___ be - come clear,

Through His love the Lord pro - vid - ed ___ a place for us to rest,

a place to find the an - swer ___ in ho - urs of dis - tress.

Now there is nev - er ___ an-y rea - son for you to give up ___ in de-spair;

Just look a - way and breathe His name, ___ He will come and meet you there.

**D.S. al Coda**

Gbmaj7/Ab  Ab7b9

In the

**CODA**

Db

King, of the

A7    Gmaj7/A  A7b9    D

King!    In    the    pres - ence _____ of Je -

F#m    B7b9    Em7

ho - vah. _____ God Al - might - y, _____

A9    D    G/A    Abmaj7/Bb  Bb7b9

_____ Prince of Peace; _____ Trou - bles

Eb    Gm

van - ish _____ hearts are mend - ed

C7b9    Fm7

_____ in the pres - ence _____

Abm6    Eb/Bb

_____ of the King;    In the

Fm7  Gm7  Abm  Fm7b5  Eb

pres - ence of the King! _____

# IN TIMES LIKE THESE

## Words and Music by RUTH CAYE JONES

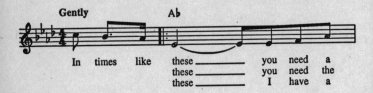

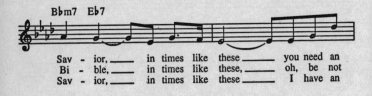

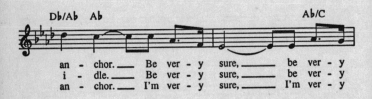

115

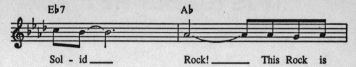

Sol - id ___ Rock! ___ This Rock is

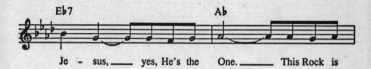

Je - sus, ___ yes, He's the One. ___ This Rock is

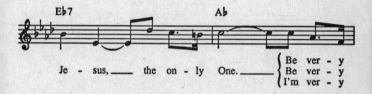

Je - sus, ___ the on - ly One. ___
Be ver - y
Be ver - y
I'm ver - y

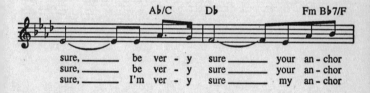

sure, ___ be ver - y sure ___ your an - chor
sure, ___ be ver - y sure ___ your an - chor
sure, ___ I'm ver - y sure ___ my an - chor

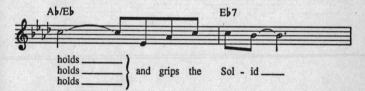

holds ___
holds ___ } and grips the Sol - id ___
holds ___

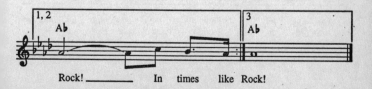

1, 2
Rock! ___ In times like
3
Rock!

# IT IS NO SECRET
## (What God Can Do)

**Words and Music by STUART HAMBLEN**

*With an easy flow*

The chimes of time ring out the news; an-
is no night, for in His light you'll

oth - er day is through. Some - one slipped and
nev - er walk a - lone. Al - ways feel at

fell; Was that some - one you? You
home, wher - ev - er you may roam. There

may have longed for add - ed strength, your
is no pow'r can con - quer you while

cour - age to re - new. Do not be dis -
God in on your side. Just take Him at His

# IT'S BEGINNING TO RAIN

**Words by GLORIA GAITHER and AARON WILBURN**
**Music by WILLIAM J. GAITHER and AARON WILBURN**

With an easy flow

It's be-gin-ning to rain _____ hear the voice of the Fa - ther _____ say-ing, "Who - so - ev - er will, come drink of this wa - ter; _____ I have prom - ised to pour my Spir - it out on your sons and your daugh - ters." _____ If you're thirst - y and dry, look up to the sky, it's be - gin - ning to rain.

C       Cmaj7

1. The tur - tle dove is
2. The young man's eyes start to
3. *(See additional lyrics)*

C7   C#dim7    G7

sing-ing its sweet song of morn-ing; _____ The
shine as he tells of his vi - sion; _____ The

Dm            G7

leaves on the trees turn their sil - ver cups to the
old un-der-stands what he sees for he's dreamed his

C          Cmaj7

sky. _____ The si - lent clouds a -
dreams. _____ With the thrill of be-ing a -

C6   C#dim7    G7

bove are be-gin-ning to gath-er; _____ The
live they reach for each oth - er; _____ And they

                    C   F

bar - ren land is thirst-y and so am I. _____
dance in the rain with the joy of the things that they've seen. _____

**D.S. al Coda**
**(3rd time)**
C

It's be-gin-ning to

**CODA**
C   F    C

rain. _____

*Additional Lyrics*

3. At the first drop of rain that you hear, throw open the windows;
Go call all your children together and throw wide the door,
When the rains of the Spirit are falling, fill ev'ry vessel,
For he who drinks his fill will thirst no more.

# JESUS DIED FOR ME

### Words and Music by
### HANK WILLIAMS

**Moderately**

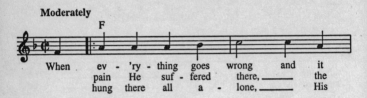

When ev-'ry-thing goes wrong and it
pain He suf-fered there, the
hung there all a - lone, His

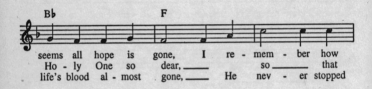

seems all hope is gone, I re-mem-ber how
Ho - ly One so dear, so that
life's blood al - most gone, He nev - er stopped

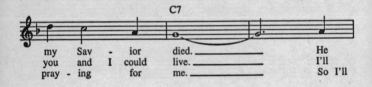

my Sav - ior died. He
you and I could live. I'll
pray - ing for me. So I'll

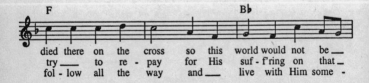

died there on the cross so this world would not be
try to re - pay for His suf - f'ring on that
fol - low all the way and live with Him some -

# JESUS IS CALLING

### Words and Music by HANK WILLIAMS and CHARLIE MONROE

**Moderately**

When your soul is wea-ry and it seems you've lost your
If you're lost in sin, — there's no need for you to

way, Je-sus is call-ing, call-ing night and
stay; Je-sus is call-ing, call-ing night and

day. When you need a friend to go with you all the
day. If the night is dark, you will soon see — the

way, Je-sus is call-ing, call-ing night and
day; Je-sus is call-ing, call-ing night and

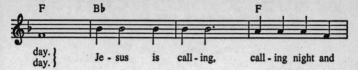

day. }
day. } Je - sus is call - ing, call - ing night and

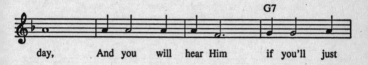

day, And you will hear Him if you'll just

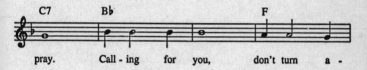

pray. Call - ing for you, don't turn a -

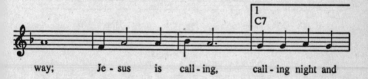

way; Je - sus is call - ing, call - ing night and

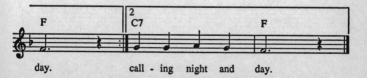

day. call - ing night and day.

# JESUS IS THE SWEETEST NAME I KNOW

### Words and Music by LELA LONG

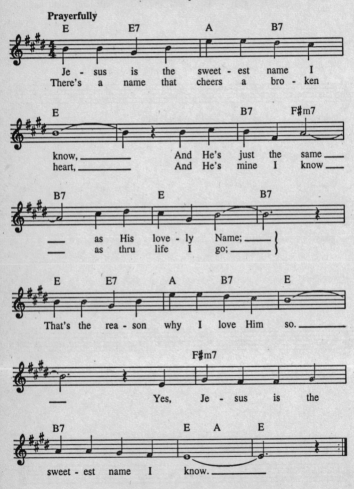

**Prayerfully**

Je-sus is the sweet-est name I know, _____ And He's just the same _____ as His love-ly Name; _____

There's a name that cheers a bro-ken heart, _____ And He's mine I know _____ as thru life I go; _____

That's the rea-son why I love Him so. _____ Yes, Je-sus is the sweet-est name I know. _____

# JUST A CLOSER WALK WITH THEE

Traditional
Arranged by KENNETH MORRIS

# JUST A LITTLE
# TALK WITH JESUS

### Words and Music by CLEAVANT DERRICKS

Moderately fast

I once was lost in sin but with—
times my path seems drear, with my—
may have doubts and fears, my

Je - sus took me in, And
out a ray of cheer, And
eyes be filled with tears, But

then a lit - tle light from heav - en filled my soul. _____ It
then a cloud of doubt may hide the light of day; _____ The
Je - sus is a friend who watch - es day and night. _____ I

bathed my heart in love and wrote my name a - bove, And
mists of sin may rise and hide the star - ry skies, But
go to Him in pray'r; He knows my ev - 'ry care, And

just a lit - tle talk with Je - sus made me
just a lit - tle talk with Je - sus clears the
just a lit - tle talk with Je - sus makes it

# JUST OVER IN
# THE GLORYLAND

**Words and Music by J.W. ACUFF and EMMETT DEAN**

# THE KING IS COMING

Words by WILLIAM J. and GLORIA GAITHER
and CHARLES MILLHUFF
Music by WILLIAM J. GAITHER

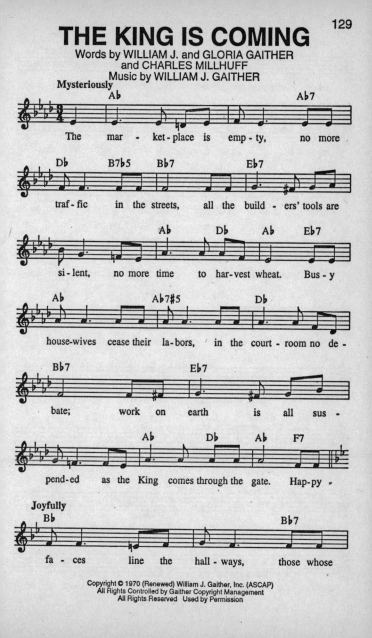

Mysteriously

The mar - ket - place is emp - ty, no more traf - fic in the streets, all the build - ers' tools are si - lent, no more time to har - vest wheat. Bus - y house-wives cease their la - bors, in the court - room no de - bate; work on earth is all sus - pend - ed as the King comes through the gate. Hap - py

Joyfully

fa - ces line the hall - ways, those whose

130

# THE KING OF WHO I AM

Words and Music by TANYA GOODMAN and MICHAEL SYKES

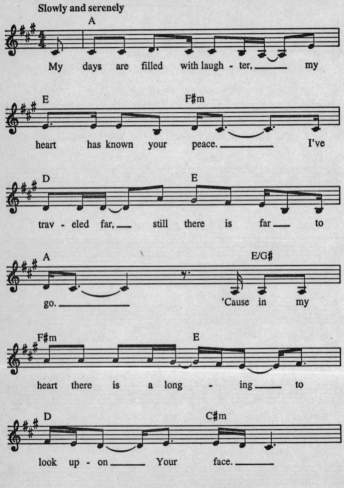

Slowly and serenely

My days are filled with laugh - ter, ____ my heart has known your peace. ____ I've trav - eled far, ____ still there is far ____ to go. ____ 'Cause in my heart there is a long - ing ____ to look up - on ____ Your face. ____

Where You are    is where    I    want    to

be. ____    You ____ are    my    King; ____

You are    the Lamb; ____    Li - on of Ju - dah,

seed    of    A - bra - ham, ____    the

Ho - ly    One, ____    God's - on - ly Son.    You

are ____    the    King ____ of    who    I ____

am.    (Instrumental)

Ev - 'ry ____

# MOVIN' UP
# TO GLORYLAND

Words and Music by
LEE ROY ABERNATHY

I love to think a-bout a par-a-dise __
I made my res-er-va-tion long a-go __

some-where be-yond the blue, _____
the day I gave up sin, _____

A man-sion wait-ing in the dis-tant skies __
And when my man-sion's read-y, this I know: __

may be next door to you; __
I'm gon-na move right in; __

136

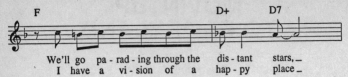

We'll go pa - rad - ing through the dis - tant stars, ⏤
I have a vi - sion of a hap - py place ⏤

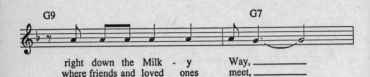

right down the Milk - y Way, ⏤⏤⏤
where friends and loved ones meet, ⏤⏤⏤

The plan - ets, Ju - pi - ter and Nep - tune and Mars ⏤
Right on the cor - ner of God's Av - e - nue ⏤

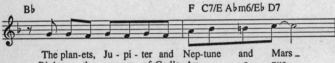

won't e - ven be half way! }
and Hal - le - lu - jah Street. }

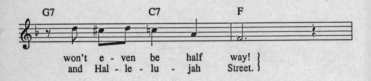

Mov - ing, mov - ing,

mov - ing up to Glo - ry - land, Mov - ing,

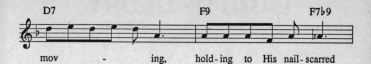

mov - ing, hold-ing to His nail-scarred

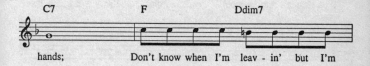

hands; Don't know when I'm leav - in' but I'm

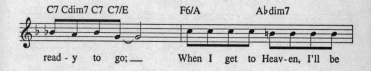

read - y to go; ___ When I get to Heav-en, I'll be

wel - come, I know, ___ Mov - ing,

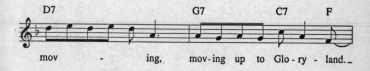

mov - ing, mov-ing up to Glo-ry - land. ___

# LAMB OF GLORY

**Words and Music by GREG NELSON
and PHILL McHUGH**

Hear the sto-ry from God's Word that kings and priests and proph-ets heard: there would be a sac-ri-fice and blood would flow to pay sin's price. Pre-cious Lamb of glo-ry, love's most won-d'rous sto-ry, heart of God's re-demp-tion of man,

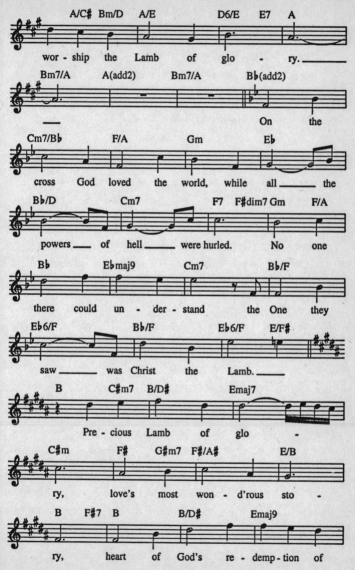

# LIFE'S RAILWAY TO HEAVEN

Words and Music by M.E. ABBEY

143

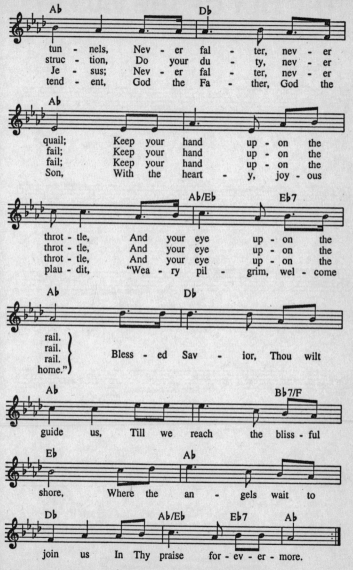

# THE LILY OF THE VALLEY

Words by CHARLES W. FRY
Music by WILLIAM S. HAYS

Gm/Bb  F/C  C7

need    to    cleanse   and   make   me   ful - ly
heart,   and   now   He   keeps   me   by   His
man - na   He   my   hun - gry   soul   shall

F       F7/A   Bb

whole.          In    sor - row He's my com - fort,   in
pow'r.          Though   all   the world for - sake me   and
fill.           Then   sweep - ing up to   glo - ry   I'll

F

trou - ble   He's   my   stay,        He ____
Sa - tan   tempt   me   sore,        Through ____
see   His   bless - ed   face        Where ____

C

tells me   ev - 'ry care on Him to   roll. }
Je - sus   I   shall safe - ly reach the   goal. }   He's the
riv - ers   of   de - light shall ev - er   roll. }

F                Bb        F

Lil - y   of the Val - ley,   the Bright and Morn-ing Star,   He's the

Gm/Bb  F/C  C7

fair - est   of   ten   thou - sand   to   my

| 1,2     |   | 3     |
| F       |   | F     |

soul.        { He ____
             { He ____ will    soul.

# LITTLE IS MUCH
# WHEN GOD IS IN IT

Words by MRS. F.W. SUFFIELD and DWIGHT BROCK
Music by MRS. F.W. SUFFIELD

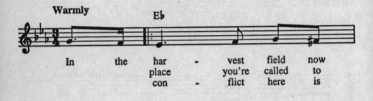

In the har - vest field now
place you're called to
con - flict here is

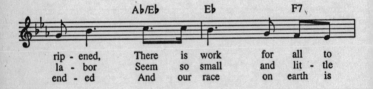

rip - ened, There is work for all to
la - bor Seem so small and lit - tle
end - ed And our race on earth is

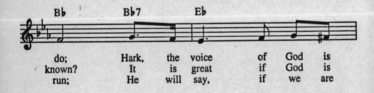

do; Hark, the voice of God is
known? It is great if God is
run; He will say, if we are

# THE LONGER I SERVE HIM

## Words and Music by WILLIAM J. GAITHER

sweet - er He grows. ___ The long - er I

serve Him, the sweet - er He grows; ___ The

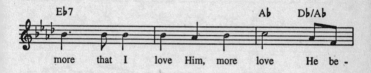

more that I love Him, more love He be -

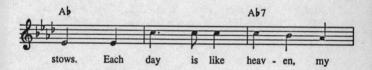

stows. Each day is like heav - en, my

heart o - ver - flows; The long - er I

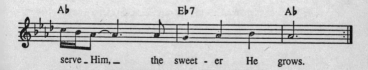

serve _ Him, _ the sweet - er He grows.

# THE LOVE OF GOD

Words and Music by FREDERICK M. LEHMAN

**Warmly**

The love of God is great-er far ___ Than tongue or
time shall pass a - way ___ And earth - ly
ink the o - cean fill, ___ And were the

pen can ev - er tell; It goes be -
thrones and king - doms fall, When men, who
skies of parch - ment made, Were ev - 'ry

yond the high - est star ___ And reach - es
here re - fuse to pray, ___ On rocks and
stalk on earth a quill, ___ And ev - 'ry

to the low - est hell. The guilt - y
hills and moun - tains call; God's love so
man a scribe by trade; To write the

pair, bowed down with care, ___ God gave His
sure shall still en - dure, ___ All mea - sure -
love of God a - bove ___ Would drain the

# MANSION OVER THE HILLTOP

Words and Music by IRA STANPHILL

**With an easy flow**

I'm sat - is - fied with   just a cot - tage be -
tempt - ed,   tor - ment-ed and
poor   or   de - sert-ed or

low, ___   A lit - tle sil - ver   and a lit - tle
test - ed,   And like the proph - et,   my __ pil - low a
lone - ly;   I'm not dis - cour - aged,   I'm __ heav - en -

gold.   But in that cit - y   where the ran - somed will
stone,   And tho' I find here   no __ per - ma - nent
bound.   I'm just a pil - grim   in __ search of a

shine, ___   I want a gold one   that's sil - ver -
dwell - ing,   I know He'll give me   a man-sion my
cit - y;   I want a man - sion,   a harp and a

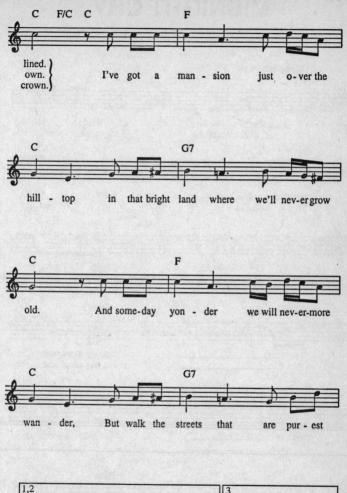

C  F/C  C          F

lined.
own.  }   I've got a man - sion    just  o - ver the
crown.

C                  G7

hill - top    in that bright land  where  we'll nev-er grow

C                  F

old.        And some-day yon - der    we will nev-er-more

C                  G7

wan - der,  But walk the streets  that   are pur - est

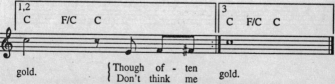

1,2
C      F/C    C

gold.      { Though of - ten
           { Don't think  me    gold.

3
C   F/C   C

# MIDNIGHT CRY

### Words and Music by GREG DAY and CHUCK DAY

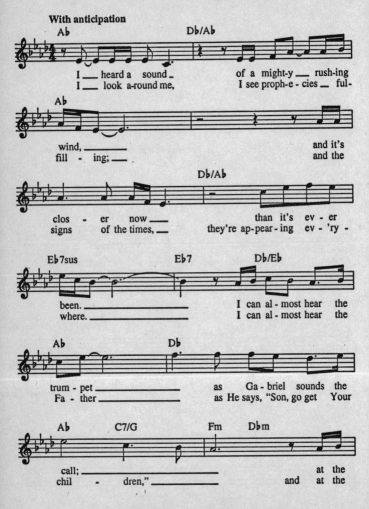

155

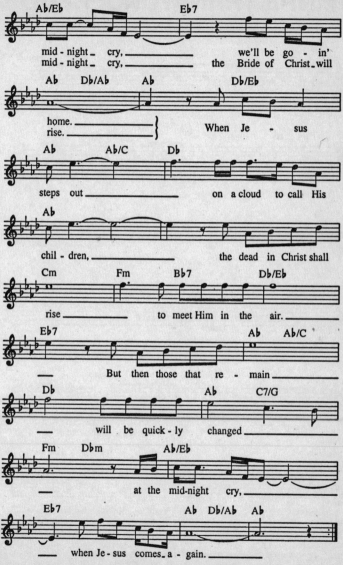

# MORE THAN WONDERFUL

### Words and Music by LANNY WOLFE

158

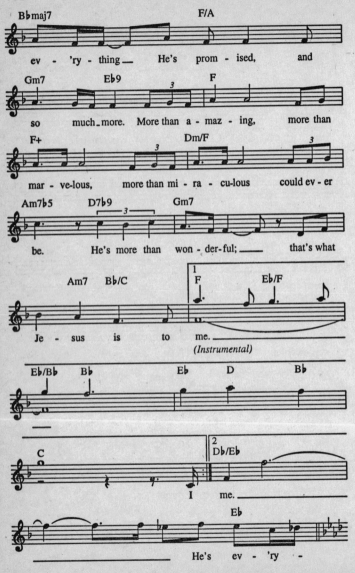

# MY GOD IS REAL
## (Yes, God Is Real)

### Words and Music by KENNETH MORRIS

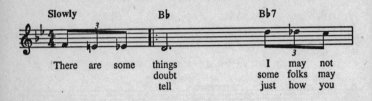

There are some things I may not
doubt some folks may
tell just how you

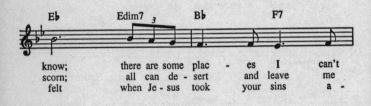

know; there are some plac - es I can't
scorn; all can de - sert and leave me
felt when Je - sus took your sins a -

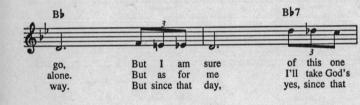

go, But I am sure of this one
alone. But as for me I'll take God's
way. But since that day, yes, since that

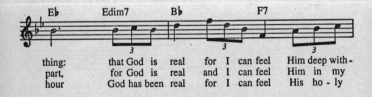

thing: that God is real for I can feel Him deep with-
part, for God is real and I can feel Him in my
hour God has been real for I can feel His ho - ly

# MY SAVIOR FIRST OF ALL

Words by FANNY J. CROSBY
Music by JOHN R. SWENEY

Reverently

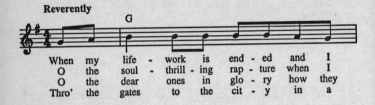

When my life-work is end-ed and I
O the soul-thrill-ing rap-ture when I
O the dear ones in glo-ry how they
Thro' the gates to the cit-y in a

cross the swell-ing tide, When the
view His bless-ed face And the
beck-on me to come, And our
robe of spot-less white, He will

bright and glo-rious morn-ing I shall
lus-ter of His kind-ly beam-ing
part-ing at the riv-er I re-
lead me where no tears will ev-er

see; I shall know my Re-deem-er when I
eye; How my full heart will praise Him for the
call; To the sweet vales of E-den they will
fall; In the glad song of a-ges I shall

# MY TRIBUTE

### Words and Music by ANDRAÉ CROUCH

How can I say thanks for the things You have done for me? Things so un-de-served, yet You give to prove Your love for me. The voic-es of a mil-lion an-gels could not ex-press my grat-i-tude. All that I am and ev-er hope to be,

done. Just let me live my life; ___ let it be pleas - ing, Lord, to Thee. ___ And should I gain an - y praise, let it go to Cal - va - ry. With HIs blood He has saved me, with His pow'r He has raised me, to God be the glo - ry for the things He has done.

# NOW I BELONG TO JESUS

Words and Music by NORMAN J. CLAYTON

**Moderately fast**

G      Am      D7

Je - sus, my Lord, will love me for - ev - er.
Once I was lost in sin's deg - ra - da - tion;
Joy floods my soul, for Je - sus has saved me,

G      Am      D7

From Him no pow'r of e - vil can sev - er.
Je - sus came down to bring me sal - va - tion,
Freed me from sin that long had en - slaved me;

B      Em      A      D      Em      A7

He gave His life to ran - som my soul; Now I be - long to
Lift - ed me up from sor - row and shame; Now I be - long to
His pre - cious blood He gave to re - deem. Now I be - long to

D7      G      Am7      D7

Him.
Him.      Now I be - long to Je - sus,
Him.

G      Bm7b5      E

Je - sus be - longs to me; Not for the years of

Am/C      C#dim7      G/D      A      D7      G

time a - lone, But for e - ter - ni - ty.

# A NEW NAME IN GLORY

Words and Music by C. AUSTIN MILES

With joy!

I was once a sin - ner, but I came,
I was hum - bly kneel - ing at the cross,
In the Book 'tis writ - ten, "Saved by grace."

Par - don to re - ceive from my Lord. _____
Fear - ing naught but God's an - gry frown, _____
O, the joy that came to my soul! _____

This was free - ly giv - en, and I found
When the heav - ens o - pened and I saw
Now I am for - giv - en, and I know

That He al - ways kept His word. )
That my name was writ - ten down. }  There's a
By the blood I am made whole. )

new name writ-ten down _ in glo - ry, _____  And it's

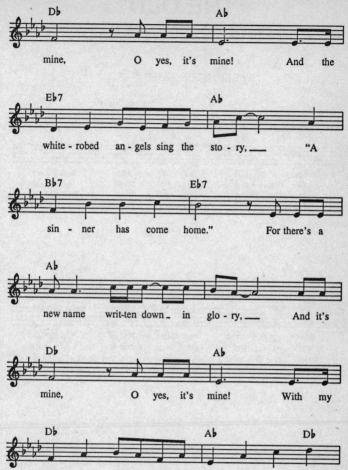

mine,      O   yes,   it's   mine!      And    the

white - robed   an - gels   sing   the   sto - ry, ___     "A

sin - ner   has   come   home."      For there's a

new   name   writ-ten down _ in   glo - ry, ___     And it's

mine,      O   yes,   it's   mine!      With    my

sins   for - giv - en   I   am   bound   for   heav - en,

Nev - er - more   to   roam.

# THE OLD RUGGED CROSS

## By REV. GEORGE BENNARD

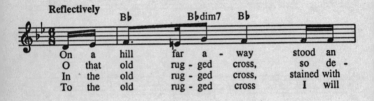

Reflectively

Bb    Bbdim7    Bb

On   a   hill   far - a - way   stood   an
O   that   old   rug - ged   cross,   so   de -
In   the   old   rug - ged   cross,   stained with
To   the   old   rug - ged   cross   I   will

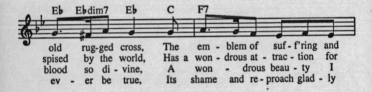

Eb   Ebdim7   Eb    C    F7

old   rug-ged   cross,   The   em - blem of   suf - f'ring and
spised   by   the   world,   Has a   won - drous at - trac - tion   for
blood   so   di - vine,   A   won - drous beau - ty   I
ev - er   be   true,   Its   shame   and re - proach glad - ly

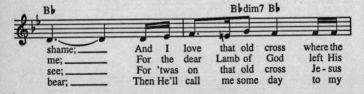

Bb                    Bbdim7   Bb

shame;____   And   I   love   that   old   cross   where the
me;____   For   the   dear   Lamb of   God   left His
see;____   For 'twas   on   that   old   cross   Je - sus
bear;____   Then He'll   call   me   some   day   to   my

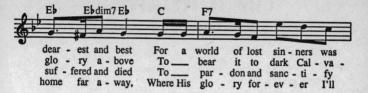

dear - est and best    For a world    of lost  sin - ners was
glo - ry a - bove    To ___  bear  it to  dark  Cal - va -
suf - fered and died    To ___  par - don and  sanc - ti - fy
home  far a - way,  Where His  glo - ry for - ev - er  I'll

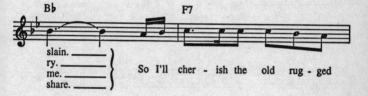

slain. _____
ry. _____
me. _____
share. _____
So I'll cher - ish the   old   rug - ged

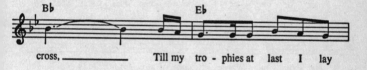

cross, _____    Till my  tro - phies at  last   I   lay

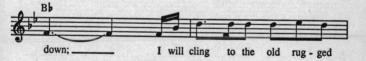

down; _____    I will cling  to the  old  rug - ged

cross, _____    And ex-change it some day  for a   crown. ___

# ON JORDAN'S STORMY BANKS

Words by SAMUEL STENNETT
American Folk Hymn
Arranged by RIGDON M. McINTOSH

With spirit

On _ Jor- dan's storm - y banks I stand, _ And cast a wish - ful eye To _ Ca- naan's_ fair and hap- py land, Where _ my pos - ses - sions lie.
All _ o'er those wide _ ex - tend - ed plains Shines one e - ter - nal day; There _ God the _ Son for- ev - er reigns And _ scat - ters_ night a - way.
No _ chill - ing winds _ nor pois - 'nous breath Can reach that health - ful shore; Sick - ness and _ sor - row, pain and death Are _ felt and _ feared no more.
When _ shall I reach _ that hap - py place, _ And be for - ev - er blest? When _ shall I _ see my Fa- ther's face, And _ in His _ bos - om rest?

I am bound for the prom - ised land, _____ I am bound for the prom - ised land; O who will _ come and go with me? I am bound for the prom - ised land.

# PRECIOUS MEMORIES

### Words and Music by J.B.F. WRIGHT

Slowly

Pre - cious mem-'ries, un - seen an - gels,
Pre - cious fa - ther, lov - ing moth - er,

Sent from some-where to my soul;
Fly a - cross the lone - ly years;

How they lin - ger, ev - er near me,
To old home-scenes of my child-hood,

And the sa - cred past un - fold.
With fond mem-o - ries ap - pear. Pre - cious mem-'ries,

how they lin - ger, How they ev - er flood my

soul. _____ In the still - ness

of the mid-night, Pre - cious sa-cred scenes un - fold.

# (There'll Be)
# PEACE IN THE VALLEY
## (For Me)

Words and Music by
THOMAS A. DORSEY

# A PERFECT HEART

### Words and Music by REBA FAYE RAMBO and DONY McGUIRE

**Moderately slow**

Morn-ing sun, light of cre - a - tion; grass-y

fields, a vel - vet floor; _____ sil-ver

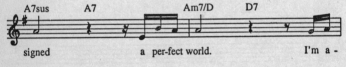

clouds, a shim-mer-ing cur - tain; He's de -

signed a per-fect world. I'm a -

mazed at His tal - ents, stand in

awe of One so great. _____ Now my _

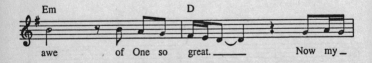

# PRECIOUS LORD, TAKE MY HAND

**(Take My Hand, Precious Lord)**

Words and Music by THOMAS A. DORSEY

# PUT YOUR HAND IN THE HAND

Words and Music by GENE MacLELLAN

Put your hand in the hand of the Man who stilled the wa - ter, _____ Put your hand in the hand of the Man who calmed the sea. _____ Take a look at your - self and - a you can look at oth - ers dif - f'rent - ly, By put - tin' your hand in the hand of the Man from Gal - i - lee. _____ {Ev - 'ry time I look in - to the / Ma - ma taught me how to pray be - fore I

# RISE AGAIN

### Words and Music by DALLAS HOLM

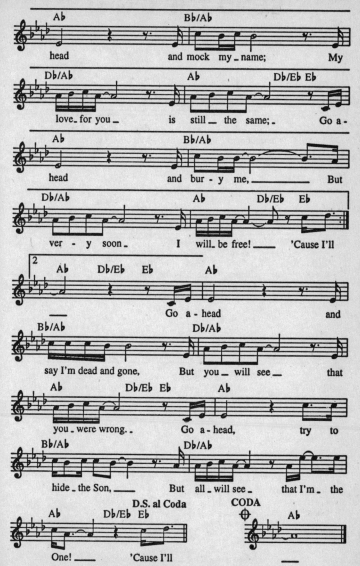

# SEND THE LIGHT

Words and Music by CHARLES GABRIEL

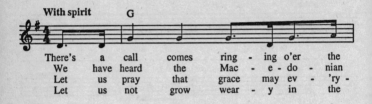

There's a call comes ring - ing o'er the
We have heard the Mac - e - do - nian
Let us pray that grace may ev - 'ry -
Let us not grow wear - y in the

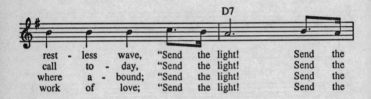

rest - less wave, "Send the light! Send the
call to - day, "Send the light! Send the
where a - bound; "Send the light! Send the
work of love; "Send the light! Send the

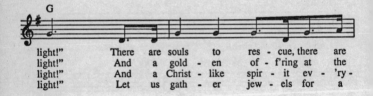

light!" There are souls to res - cue, there are
light!" And a gold - en of - f'ring at the
light!" And a Christ - like spir - it ev - 'ry -
light!" Let us gath - er jew - els for a

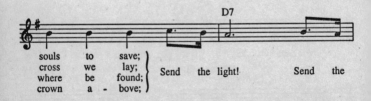

souls to save; }
cross we lay; } Send the light! Send the
where be found; }
crown a - bove; }

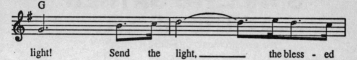

light!      Send    the    light, _____    the bless - ed

gos - pel    light;    Let    it    shine _____    from shore    to

shore!      Send    the    light, _____    the bless - ed

gos - pel       light;      Let      it

shine _____    for - ev - er - more!

# SHALL WE GATHER AT THE RIVER?

**Words and Music by ROBERT LOWRY**

Shall we gather at the river
Ere we reach the shin - ing riv - er,
Soon we'll reach the shin - ing riv - er;

Where bright an - gel feet have trod,_____
Lay we ev - 'ry bur - den down;_____
Soon our pil - grim - age will cease;_____

With its crys - tal tide for - ev - er Flow - ing
Grace our spir - its will de - liv - er And pro -
Soon our hap - py hearts will quiv - er With the

by the throne of ___ God? }
vide us a robe and a crown. }    Yes, we'll gath - er at the
mel - o - dy of ___ peace. }

riv - er, The beau - ti - ful, the beau - ti - ful ___

riv - er, Gath - er with the saints ___ at the

riv - er That flows by the throne of ___ God.

# SWEET BY AND BY

**Words and Music by S. FILLMORE BENNETT
and JOSEPH P. WEBSTER**

Prayerfully

There's a land that is fair-er than day And by
boun-ti-ful Fa-ther a-bove, We will

faith we can see it a-far, For the
of-fer our trib-ute of praise For the

Fa-ther waits o-ver the way To pre-
glo-ri-ous gift of His love And the

pare us a dwell-ing place there.) In the
bless-ings that hal-low our days.)

sweet by and by, We shall meet on that beau-ti-ful

shore. In the sweet by and by, We shall

meet on that beau-ti-ful shore. To our shore.

# SHELTERED IN THE ARMS OF GOD

**Words and Music by DOTTIE RAMBO and JIMMIE DAVIS**

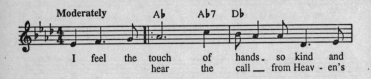

I feel the touch of the hands so kind and
hear the call from Heav-en's

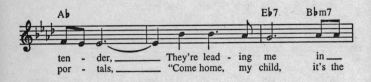

ten-der, _____ They're lead-ing me in _____
por-tals, _____ "Come home, my child, it's the

paths that I must trod; _____ I have no
last mile you must trod;" _____ I'll fall a-

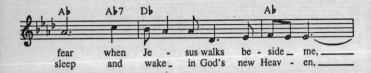

fear when Je-sus walks be-side me,
sleep and wake in God's new Heav-en,

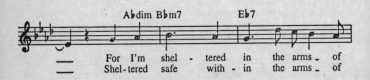

_____ For I'm shel-tered in the arms of
_____ Shel-tered safe with-in the arms of

# SOMETHING BEAUTIFUL

### Words by GLORIA GAITHER
### Music by WILLIAM J. GAITHER

# SOON AND VERY SOON

**Words and Music by ANDRAÉ CROUCH**

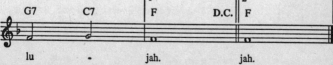

Bb

Soon and ver - y soon ___
No more cry - in' there, ___
No more dy - in' there, ___
we are

F

goin' to see the King. ___ Hal - le -

F7    Bb                Gm7b5

lu - jah, ___ Hal - le - lu - jah, ___ we're

F/C    C7  F    [1]        [2,3]

goin' to see the King! ___ ___ Hal - le -

G7    C7    F              G7    C7

lu - jah, Hal - le - lu -

F              G7    C7    F

jah, Hal - le - lu - jah, Hal - le -

G7    C7    [1] F    D.C.    [2] F

lu - jah.              jah.

# 194
# STEPPING ON THE CLOUDS

## Words and Music by LINDA STALLS

One of these days _____ I'm gon - na
moon _____ the stars and the

leave _____ One of these days _____ I'm go - ing
plan - ets I'm gon - na walk _____ on the milk - y white

home _____ I'm gon - na take my fi - nal
way _____ When ole Ga - briel _____ gives the

jour - ney _____ I'm gon - na rest _____ 'neath heav - en's blue
sig - nal _____ I'm gon - na leave _____ for heav - en to

dome. }
stay. }     Step - ping on the clouds we'll see Je - sus

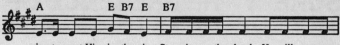

rise to meet Him in the air, Step-ping on the clouds He will greet us,

oh, the joy to - geth - er we'll share ___

___ I'm gon-na leave this world be-hind me go-ing where the

dev - il can - not find me I'm go - ing

high - er high - er high - er ___

___ Step-ping on ___ the

1. clouds.  2. Go-ing past the clouds.

# SURELY THE PRESENCE OF THE LORD IS IN THIS PLACE

### Words and Music by LANNY WOLFE

# SWING DOWN CHARIOT

## Traditional Spiritual

With energy

**F** Why don't you swing down, char-i-ot, stop and

**C** let me ride? _____ Swing down, char-i-ot, stop and

**F7/A** **Bb** let me ride. _____ Rock me, Lord, rock me, Lord,

**F** **Dm7** **G7** **To Coda** calm and eas - y. I've got a home on the

**C7** **F** oth - er side. Well, _____ E - / Well, _____ E -

ze - ki - el _____ went down in the / ze - ki - el _____ went down and he

mid - dle of ____ the field. He
got ___ on _____ board, The

saw an an - gel work - in' on a
char - i - ot went a - bump - in' on ___

char - i - ot wheel. ___ He
down that old road. ___ He

was - n't par - tic - u - lar 'bout the
was - n't par - tic - u - lar 'bout the

char - i - ot wheel, _____ He
bump - in' of the road, ___ He

N.C.

just want - ed to see how the
just want - ed to lay down his

1

char - i - ot feels. ___ Why don't you

200

D.S. al Coda

heav - y load.____ Why don't you

CODA

C7          F

oth - er side. Why don't you

swing down, char - i - ot, stop and

C

let me ride?____ Swing down, char-i-ot, stop and

F7          Bb

let me ride.____ Rock me, Lord, rock me, Lord,

F          Dm7          G7

calm and eas - y. I've got a home on the

Am/C          F

oth - er side.

# THERE IS POWER
# IN THE BLOOD

Words and Music by LEWIS E. JONES

**Brightly**

Would you be free from the bur-den of sin? There's
Would you be free from your pas-sion and pride? There's
Would you be whit-er, much whit-er than snow? There's
Would you do ser-vice for Je-sus your King? There's

pow'r in the blood, pow'r in the blood;
pow'r in the blood, pow'r in the blood;
pow'r in the blood, pow'r in the blood;
pow'r in the blood, pow'r in the blood;

Would you o'er e-vil a vic-to-ry win?
Come for a cleans-ing to Cal-va-ry's tide;
Sin stains are lost in its life giv-ing flow;
Would you live dai-ly His prais-es to sing

There's

won-der-ful pow'r in the blood. There is

pow'r, pow'r, won-der-work-ing pow'r in the

blood of the Lamb; There is pow'r, pow'r,

won-der-work-ing pow'r in the pre-cious blood of the Lamb.

# SWING LOW, SWEET CHARIOT

African-American Spiritual

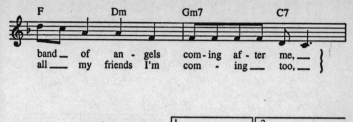

band _ of an - gels com - ing af - ter me, _
all _ my friends I'm com - ing _ too, _

Com-ing for to car-ry me home. home.

Swing low, sweet char - i - ot, _

Com - ing for to car - ry me home.

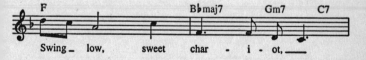

Swing _ low, sweet char - i - ot, _

Com - ing for to car - ry me home.

204

# THERE'S SOMETHING ABOUT THAT NAME

Words by WILLIAM J. and GLORIA GAITHER
Music by WILLIAM J. GAITHER

**Moderately**

Je - sus,   Je - sus,   Je -

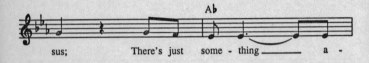

sus;   There's just some - thing _____ a -

bout   that   name! _____

Mas - ter,   Sav - ior,   Je -

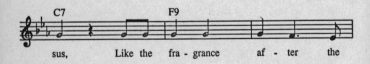

sus,   Like the fra - grance af - ter the

rain. _____ Je - sus,

Je - sus, Je - sus, Let all

Heav - en _____ and earth pro -

claim: _____ Kings and

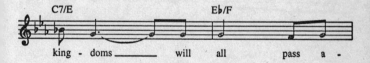

king - doms _____ will all pass a -

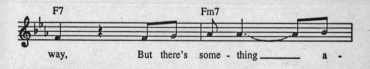

way, But there's some - thing _____ a -

bout that name! _____

# TURN YOUR RADIO ON

### Words and Music by ALBERT BRUMLEY

**Moderately**

1. Come and lis-ten in to a ra-di-o sta-tion where the might-y
2. in to a glo-ry-land cho-rus, lis-ten to the
3. *(See additional lyrics)*

hosts of Heav-en sing, turn your ra-di-o
glad ho-san-nas roll, turn your ra-di-o

on, _____ turn your ra-di-o on; If you want to
Get a lit-tle

hear the songs of Zi-on com-ing from the
taste of joy a-wait-ing, get a lit-tle

land of end-less spring, get in touch with
Heav-en in your soul, get in touch with

God, _____ turn your ra-di-o

on. _____ Turn your ra-di-o on _____ and lis-ten to the

mu-sic in the air, turn your ra-di-o on, _____ Heav-en's glo-ry

share; _____ Turn the lights down low _____ and lis-ten to the

Mas-ter's ra-di-o, get in touch with

God, _____ turn your ra-di-o

1,2 on. Broth-er, lis-ten on.

3

### Additional Lyrics

3. Listen to the songs of the fathers and mothers
   and the many friends gone on before,
Turn your radio on, turn your radio on;
Some eternal morning we shall meet them
   over on the hallelujah shore,
Get in touch with God, turn your radio on.
*Chorus*

# UNCLOUDED DAY

### Words and Music by J.K. ALWOOD

**Brightly**

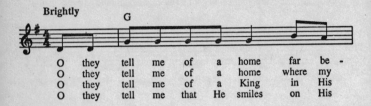

O they tell me of a home far be-
O they tell me of a home where my
O they tell me of a King in His
O they tell me that He smiles on His

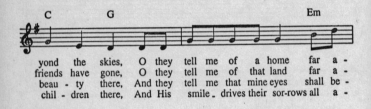

yond the skies, O they tell me of a home far a-
friends have gone, O they tell me of that land far a-
beau-ty there, And they tell me that mine eyes shall be-
chil-dren there, And His smile. drives their sor-rows all a-

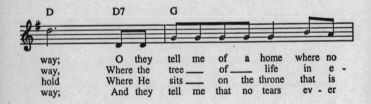

way; O they tell me of a home where no
way, Where the tree of life in e-
hold Where He sits on the throne that is
way; And they tell me that no tears ev-er

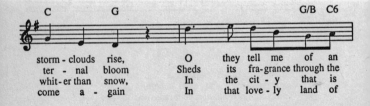

storm-clouds rise, O they tell me of an
ter-nal bloom Sheds its fra-grance through the
whit-er than snow, In the cit-y that is
come a-gain In that love-ly land of

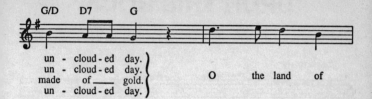

un - cloud - ed day.
un - cloud - ed day.
made of ___ gold.
un - cloud - ed day.

O the land of

cloud - less day! O the land of an

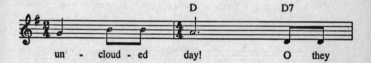

un - cloud - ed day! O they

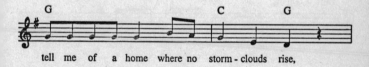

tell me of a home where no storm - clouds rise,

O they tell me of an un - cloud-ed day.

# UPON THIS ROCK

Words by GLORIA GAITHER
Music by DONY McGUIRE

When oth-ers see with earth-ly eyes just what they want to see, you will see the things that nev-er die. You will know and re-cog-nize by sim-ple child-like faith the price-less truth that oth-ers will de-ny. When oth-ers say I'm just a man who liked to dream his dreams, when oth-ers call a mir-a-cle a

sim-ple car-pen-ter you see the Son of God, if you will choose to lose when you could

**Bb(add2)  Asus  A  Dm  F/C**

myth, \_\_\_\_\_ you'll lis-ten for e-ter-ni-ty\_\_ in mo-ments
win; \_\_\_\_\_ if you will give your life\_ a-way\_ for noth-ing

**Gm9  Gsus  G7**

as they pass and see with spir-it eyes\_ what oth-ers
in re-turn, then you are where my King - dom will be-

**Eb  Bbm7  Eb9  Ab**

miss.
gin. } Up-on this Rock _____ I'll

**Bbm6/G  C  Ab/Gb**

build my King - dom up-on this Rock for-ev-er and ev - er

**Bb/F  C#m/E**

it shall stand. And all the pow'rs of hell it-self\_ shall nev-er

**Cm9  Fm7  To Coda ⊕**

more pre-vail a - gainst\_ it, for

**Ab/Bb  Bb7**

Sa-tan's thrones\_ are built \_\_ on sink-ing

**Gb  Db/Eb  Eb9  Ab**

sand. Up-on this Rock \_\_\_\_\_ I'll

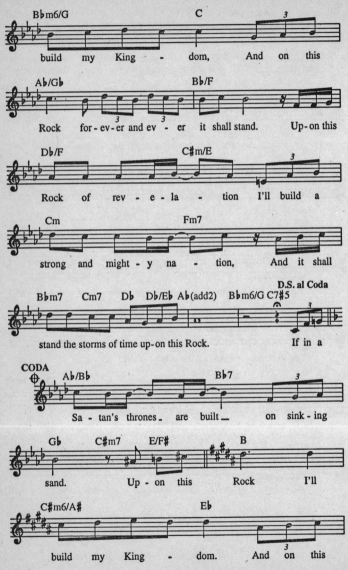

B/A

Rock for - ev - er and ev - er

C#/G#

it shall ___ stand. ___ Up - on this

F/G#     Em/G

Rock of rev - e - la - tion I'll build a

D#m     G#m

strong and might - y na - tion, And it shall

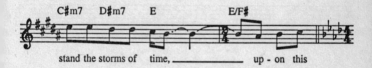

C#m7  D#m7   E     E/F#

stand the storms of time, _____ up - on this

Ab(add2)     F/A

Rock.     I'll build my King - dom, And on this

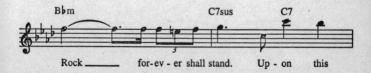

Bbm     C7sus   C7

Rock ___ for-ev - er shall stand. Up - on this

214

Rock of rev-e-la - tion I'll build a

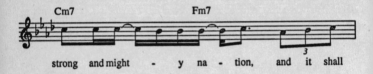

strong and might - y na - tion, and it shall

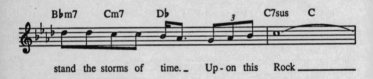

stand the storms of time.__ Up-on this Rock _____

__ I'll build my __ church up - on this

Rock, _____ up - on this

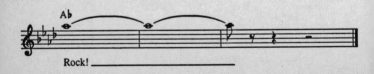

Rock! _____

# WE HAVE COME INTO HIS HOUSE

### Words and Music by BRUCE BALLINGER

**Prayerfully**

We have come in-to His house and
get a-bout our-selves and

gath-ered in His name to wor-ship Him. _____ We have
mag-ni-fy His name and wor-ship Him. _____ Let's for-

come in-to His house and gath-ered in His name to
get a-bout our-selves and mag-ni-fy His name and

wor - ship Him. _____ We have
wor - ship Him. _____ Let's for -

come in-to His house and gath-ered in His name to
get a-bout our-selves and mag-ni-fy His name and

wor-ship Christ the Lord. Wor - ship Him, Christ __ the
wor-ship Christ the Lord. Wor - ship Him, Christ __ the

**1.** Lord. _____ Let's for -  **2.** Lord. _____

# VICTORY IN JESUS

Words and Music by E.M. BARTLETT

# WE SHALL BEHOLD HIM

Words and Music by DOTTIE RAMBO

219

220

# WILL THE CIRCLE
# BE UNBROKEN

Words by ADA R. HABERSHON
Music by CHARLES H. GABRIEL

# WE'LL UNDERSTAND IT BETTER BY AND BY

### Words and Music by CHARLES A. TINDLEY

Brightly

Tri - als dark on ev - 'ry hand, And we
cher - ished plans have failed, Dis - ap -
ta - tions, hid - den snares Of - ten

can - not un - der - stand All the
point - ments have pre - vailed, And we've
take us un - a - wares, And our

ways that God would lead us to that
wan - dered in the dark - ness, heav - y -
hearts are made to bleed for some

bless - ed Prom - ised Land. But He'll
heart - ed and a - lone. But we're
thought - less word or deed; And we

guide us with His eye, And we'll fol-low till we die; We will
trust-ing in the Lord, And ac-cord-ing to His Word, We will
won-der why the test When we try to do our best, But we'll

un - der - stand it bet - ter by and by.)
un - der - stand it bet - ter by and by.
un - der - stand it bet - ter by and by.)

By and by, when the morn - ing comes,

When the saints of God are gath-ered home, We will

tell the sto - ry how we've o - ver-come; We will

un - der - stand it bet - ter by and

by. { Oft our
{ Temp - by.

# WEALTH WON'T SAVE YOUR SOUL

### Words and Music by
### HANK WILLIAMS

**Moderately**

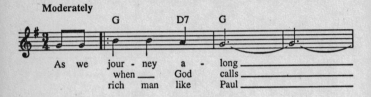

As we jour-ney a - long _____
when ___ God calls _____
rich man like Paul _____

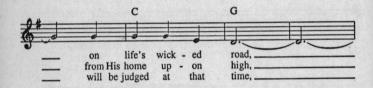

___ on life's wick - ed road, _____
___ from His home up - on high, _____
___ will be judged at that time, _____

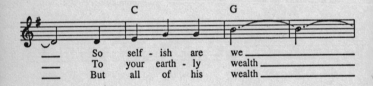

___ So self - ish are we _____
___ To your earth - ly wealth _____
___ But all of his wealth _____

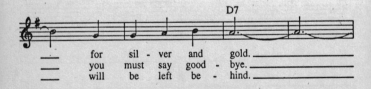

___ for sil - ver and gold. _____
___ you must say good - bye. _____
___ will be left be - hind. _____

You can treas - ure your wealth,
Then it's use - less to you
For no mat - ter how much

your dia - monds and gold;
if you've strayed from the fold;
earth - ly wealth you dear hold,

But, my friends, it won't save
For, my friends, it won't save
My friends, it won't save

your poor wick - ed soul.
your poor wick - ed soul.
your poor wick - ed soul.

1, 2
For

3
The

# WHEN GOD COMES AND GATHERS HIS JEWELS

Words and Music by
HANK WILLIAMS

**Reflectively**

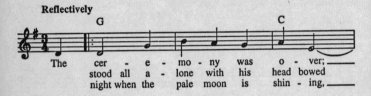

The cer - e - mo - ny was o - ver;
stood all a - lone with his head bowed
night when the pale moon is shin - ing,

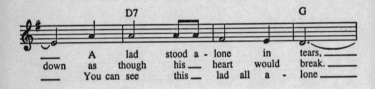

down     A lad stood a - lone in tears,
down     as though his heart would break.
You can see this lad all a - lone

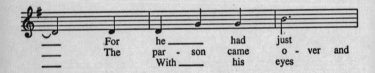

For he had just
The par - son came o - ver and
With his eyes

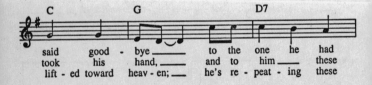

said good - bye to the one he had
took his hand, and to him these
lift - ed toward heav - en; he's re - peat - ing these

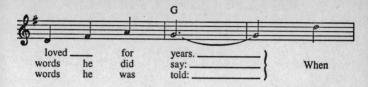

loved ___ for years: ___
words he did say: ___
words he was told: ___ When

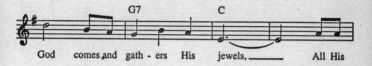

God comes and gath - ers His jewels, ___ All His

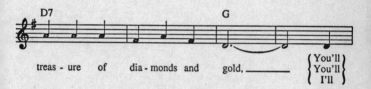

treas - ure of dia - monds and gold, ___ { You'll } { You'll } { I'll }

meet her up there, up in heav - en so

fair, When God comes and gath - ers His

1, 2
G
jewels. ___ { He } { Each }

3
G
jewels. ___

# WHEN I CAN READ
# MY TITLE CLEAR

### Words by ISAAC WATTS
### Traditional American Melody attributed to JOSEPH C. LOWRY

**Moderately**

When I can read my
Should earth, a - gainst my
Let cares like a wild
There shall I bathe my

ti - tle clear To man - sions in the
soul en - gage, And fi - ery darts be
de - luge come, And storms of sor - row
wea - ry soul In seas of heav'n - ly

skies, I'll
hurled, Then
fall! May
rest, And

bid fare - well to ev - 'ry fear And
I can smile at Sa - tan's rage And
I but safe - ly reach my home, My
not a wave of trou - ble roll A -

# WHEN THE BOOK OF LIFE IS READ

Words and Music by
**HANK WILLIAMS**

**Brightly**

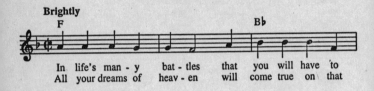

In life's man-y bat-tles that you will have to
All your dreams of heav-en will come true on that

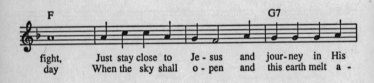

fight, Just stay close to Je-sus and jour-ney in His
day When the sky shall o-pen and this earth melt a-

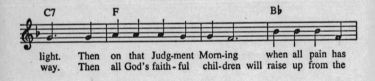

light. Then on that Judg-ment Morn-ing when all pain has
way. Then all God's faith-ful chil-dren will raise up from the

fled, You'll stand __ in God's King-dom when the
dead U-nit-ed in God's King-dom when the

# WHEN THE ROLL IS CALLED UP YONDER

**Words and Music by JAMES M. BLACK**

**Brightly**

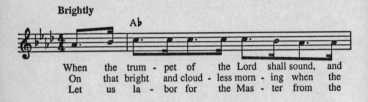

When the trum-pet of the Lord shall sound, and
On that bright and cloud-less morn-ing when the
Let us la-bor for the Mas-ter from the

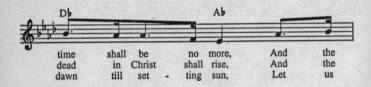

time shall be no more, And the
dead in Christ shall rise, And the
dawn till set-ting sun, Let us

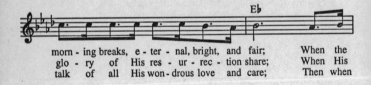

morn-ing breaks, e-ter-nal, bright, and fair; When the
glo-ry of His res-ur-rec-tion share; When His
talk of all His won-drous love and care; Then when

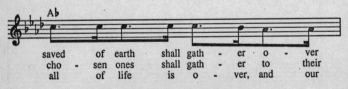

saved of earth shall gath-er o-ver
cho-sen ones shall gath-er to their
all of life is o-ver, and our

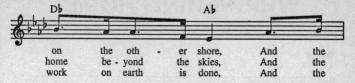

on · · the · oth - er · shore, · And · · the
home · · be - yond · the · skies, · And · · the
work · · on · earth · is · done, · And · · the

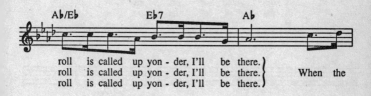

roll · is called · up yon - der, I'll · be there.
roll · is called · up yon - der, I'll · be there. · When · the
roll · is called · up yon - der, I'll · be there.

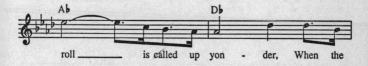

roll _____ · is called · up yon - der, · When · the

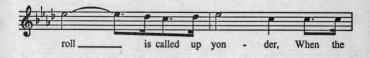

roll _____ · is called · up yon - der, · When · the

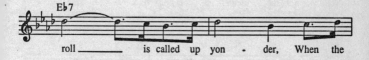

roll _____ · is called · up yon - der, · When · the

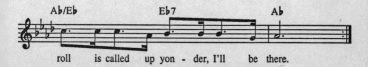

roll · is called · up yon - der, I'll · be there.

# WHISPERING HOPE

### Words and Music by ALICE HAWTHORNE

Slowly

C       F       C

Soft   as   the   voice   of   an   an - gel
If,   in   the   dusk   of   the   twi - light,
Hope,   as   an   an - chor   so   stead - fast,

G7                C

Breath - ing   a   les - son   un - heard,_____
Dim   be   the   re - gion   a - far,_____
Rends   the   dark   veil   for   the   soul,_____

F

Hope   with   a   gen - tle   per - sua - sion
Will   not   the   deep - en - ing   dark - ness
Whith - er   the   Mas - ter   has   en - tered,

C/G       G7       C

Whis - pers   her   com - fort - ing   word:_____
Bright - en   the   glim - mer - ing   star?_____
Rob - bing   the   grave   of   its   goal._____

                       Adim7   G7/B    C

Wait   till   the   dark - ness   is   o -
Then   when   the   night   is   up - on
Come   then,   O   come,   glad   fru - i -

# WHY ME?
### (Why Me, Lord?)

**Words and Music by
KRIS KRISTOFFERSON**

Moderately, with a Gospel feeling

Lord, help me, Je - sus, I've wast - ed it

so, Help me, Je - sus, I know what I

am. ___ But now that I

know that I've need - ed you, So, help me

To Coda

Je - sus, my soul's in your hands.

D.S. al Coda

Try me, Lord, hands.

CODA

hands. ___ Je - sus, my

soul's in your hands. ___

# WINGS OF A DOVE

Words and Music by BOB FERGUSON

He sends down His love _____
He sent him His love _____
He sent Him His love _____

on the wings of a dove. _____
on the wings of a dove. _____
on the wings of a dove. _____

On the wings of a snow

white dove He sends His pure

sweet love, A sign from a - bove _____

on the wings of a

dove. _____ { When No - ah had
{ When Je - sus went

dove. _____

# WONDERFUL GRACE OF JESUS

Traditional

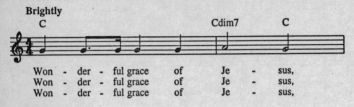

Won - der - ful grace of Je - sus,
Won - der - ful grace of Je - sus,
Won - der - ful grace of Je - sus,

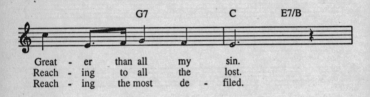

Great - er than all my sin.
Reach - ing to all the lost.
Reach - ing the most de - filed.

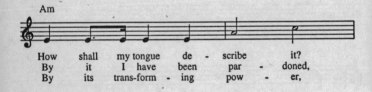

How shall my tongue de - scribe it?
By it I have been par - doned,
By its trans-form - ing pow - er,

Where shall its praise be - gin?
Saved to the ut - ter - most.
Mak - ing him God's dear child.

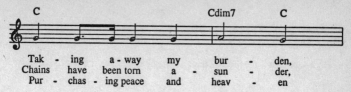

Tak - ing    a - way    my    bur - den,
Chains    have    been torn    a - sun - der,
Pur - chas - ing peace    and    heav - en

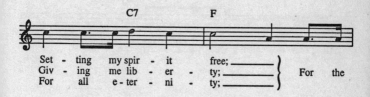

Set - ting    my spir - it    free; _____
Giv - ing    me lib - er - ty; _____    } For    the
For    all    e - ter - ni - ty; _____

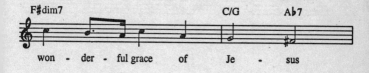

won - der - ful grace    of    Je - sus

reach - es    me.

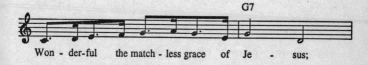

Won - der-ful    the match - less grace    of    Je - sus;

Deep - er than    the might - y roll - ing sea.

High - er than the moun - tain; spar - kling like a foun - tain;

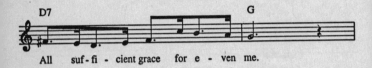

All suf - fi - cient grace for e - ven me.

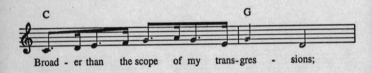

Broad - er than the scope of my trans - gres - sions;

Great - er far than all my sin and shame. O

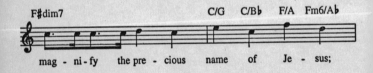

mag - ni - fy the pre - cious name of Je - sus;

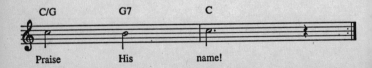

Praise His name!

# A WONDERFUL TIME UP THERE
## (Everybody's Gonna Have a Wonderful Time Up There)

Words and Music by LEE ROY ABERNATHY

Lis - ten, ev - 'ry - bod - y, 'cause I'm talk - ing to you. __ Je - sus is the on - ly one to car - ry you through. __ Now you bet - ter get you read - y for I'm

Lis - ten here, my sis - ter, we're not leav - ing you out. __ You may not be a preach - er but you sing ___ and shout. ___ What's the use to wor - ry if you've

When the trib - u - la - tions seem to dark - en the way, __ that's the time to get down on your knees ___ and pray. ___ Ev - 'ry - bod - y gon - na have their

get your Ho - ly Bi - ble in the back of the book, __ the book of Rev - e - la - tion, that's the place you must look; ___ If you un - der - stand it and you

tell-ing you why, ___ Je - sus is a-com-ing from His
been re - deemed, 'cause Heav-en's e - ven bet-ter than a
trou - bles, too. ___ Got - ta be so care-ful 'bout the
can if you try, ___ Je - sus is a - com-in' from His

Edim7   D7   G

throne on high; ___ Man - y are the wea-ry and the
mis - er dreamed; _ Think a-bout the trou-ble you could
things we do; ___ We're go-ing down the val-ley, go-ing
throne on high; ___ Read-in' in the Bi-ble all the

lone ___ and sad, _ They're gon-na wish they had-n't done the
save ___ some soul, _ Tell them what to do to reach the
one ___ by one, _ Gon-na be re-ward-ed for the
things that He said, _ Said He was a-com-in' back to

D7   G

things _ they had. _ How're you gon-na feel a-bout the
shin - ing goal, _ Sure - ly you can show them how to
things _ we've done. _ When we get to Heav-en and the
raise _ the dead, _ Are you gon-na be a-mong the

A9   D13

things He'll say ___ on that judg-ment
find the light, ___ make the whole thing
prom - ised land, ___ then we'll un - der -
cho - sen few, ___ will you make it

G

day?  ⎫
right.  ⎬   Ev - 'ry - bod - y's gon - na have re -
stand.  ⎪
through? ⎭

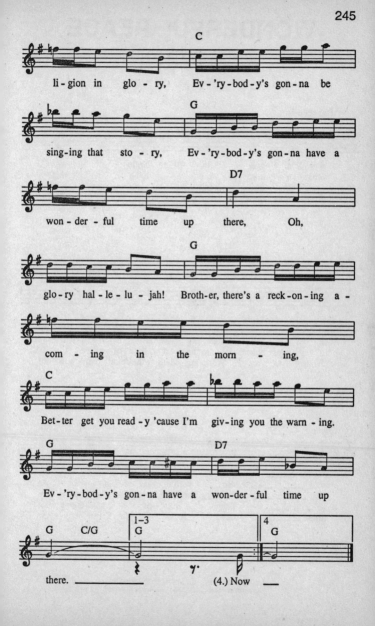

245

# WONDERFUL PEACE

Words by W.D. CORNELL
Music by W.G. COOPER

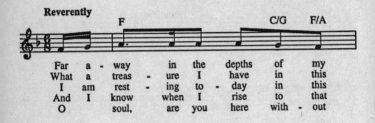

Reverently

F      C/G   F/A

Far a - way   in the depths of my
What a treas - ure I have in in this
I am rest - ing to - day in in this
And I know when I rise to that
O soul, are you here with - out

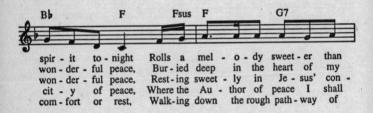

Bb    F     Fsus F    G7

spir - it to - night Rolls a mel - o - dy sweet - er than
won - der - ful peace, Bur - ied deep in the heart of my
won - der - ful peace, Rest - ing sweet - ly in Je - sus' con -
cit - y of peace, Where the Au - thor of peace I shall
com - fort or rest, Walk - ing down the rough path - way of

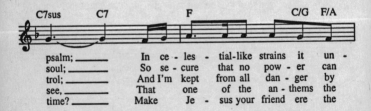

C7sus    C7      F     C/G F/A

psalm; _____ In ce - les - tial-like strains it un -
soul; _____ So se - cure that no pow - er can
trol; _____ And I'm kept from all dan - ger by
see, _____ That one of the an - thems the
time? _____ Make Je - sus your friend ere the

**Bb**    **G7/B  F/C**    **C7**

ceas - ing - ly  falls  O'er my  soul  like an  in - fi - nite
mine  it  a - way,  While the  years  of  e - ter - ni - ty
night  and  by  day,  Now His  glo - ry  is  flood - ing  my
ran - somed will sing,  In that  heav - en - ly  king - dom shall
shad - ows grow dark;  O  ac - cept  this sweet peace so  sub -

**F**        **F/A**

calm. _____
roll. _____
soul. _____     Peace!     Peace!
be: _____
lime. _____

**Bb**        **F**

won - der - ful  peace,    Com - ing

**Dm**     **G7**     **C**

down  from the  Fa - ther  a - bove, _____ Sweep -

**F**     **C/G  F/A  Bb**

o - ver my  spir - it  for - ev - er,  I  pray,  In ___

**F/C**     **C7**     **F**

fath - om - less  bil - lows  of  love. _____

# WRITTEN IN RED

Words and Music by GORDON JENSEN

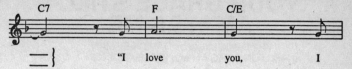

"I love you, I

love you," that's what

Cal - va - ry said. _____ "I

love you, I love _____

you, _____ I love you,"

writ - ten in red. _____

# YOUR GRACE STILL AMAZES ME

**Words and Music by DAVID LEHMAN,
TONY BROWN and KEN HARDING**

With movement

I thank You for the mer - cy
Man - y trials and heart - aches

You have shown ____ to me
I've al - read - y seen ____

With - out Your nev - er - end - ing love I
And by Your ev - er - last - ing grace, My

don't know __ where I'd be. ____ Your
soul has __ been re - deemed. _ My

pow - er al - ways lift - ed me. __ Your
life to You I free - ly give. _ My

blood has set me free. __ Though I may not un -
heart is Yours a - lone. __ You have brought me safe.

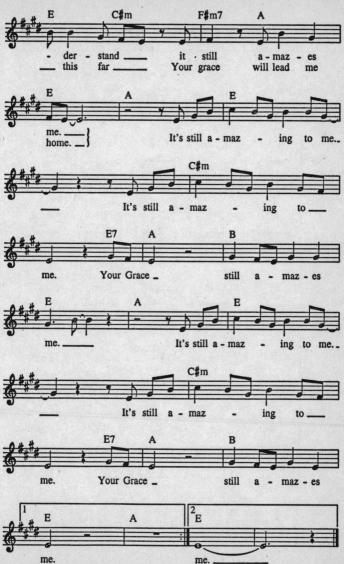

# GUITAR CHORD FRAMES

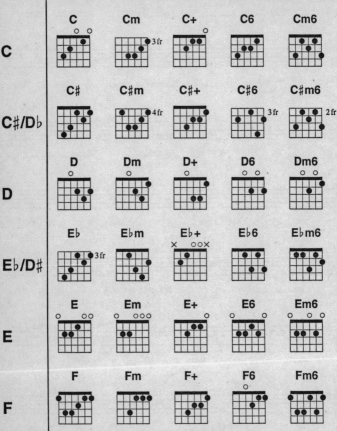

This guitar chord reference includes 120 commonly used chords. For a more complete guide to guitar chords, see "THE PAPERBACK CHORD BOOK" (HL00702009).

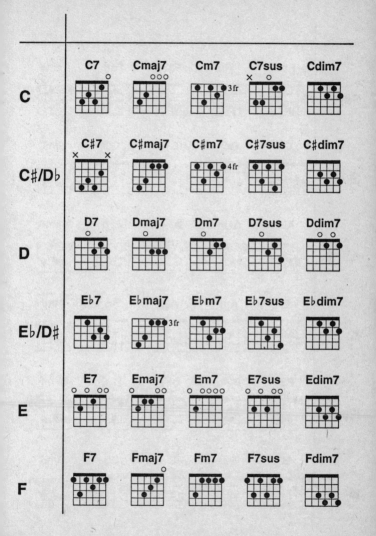

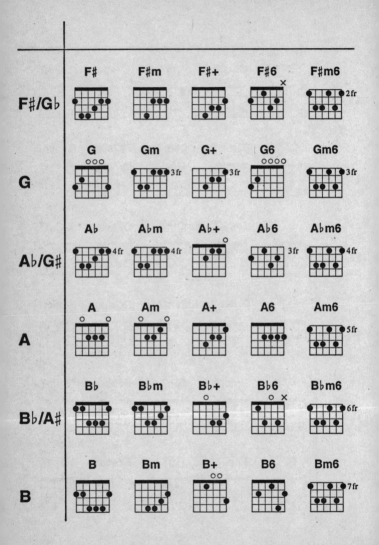

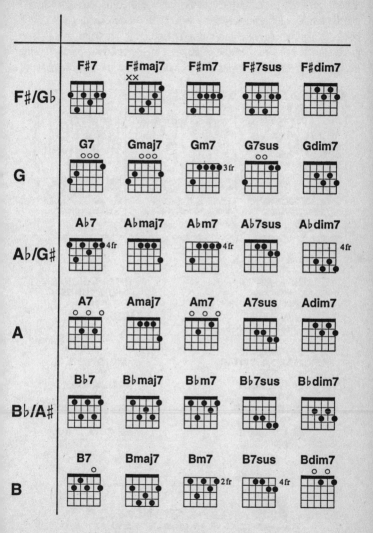